NATIONAL GEOGRAPHIC
WASHINGTON, D.C.

HEY, BABY!

A COLLECTION OF PICTURES, POEMS, AND STORIES FROM NATURE'S NURSERY

Stephanie Warren Drimmer

Contents

Introduction   6
"Good Morning"   8

MOUNTAINS AND PLAINS BABIES   10

"The Pet Rabbit"   12
Prairie Dog   14
Bison   15
Bighorn Sheep   16
To the Rescue! Bringing Up Baby Bears   18
Beaver   20
Mustang   21
Baby Buddies: Mini Mountain Lions Get Smelly Friend   22
Bobcat   24
Bald Eagle   25
Tiny Tales: Why the Porcupine Has Quills   26
Coyote   28
Tot Lot   30

RIVER AND RAIN FOREST BABIES   32

"Frog Ballet"   34
Tamandua   36
Ocelot   37
To the Rescue! Saving Sloths   38
Guanaco   40
Armadillo   42
Capybara   43
Baby Buddies: Mini Monkey Gets Cuddly Companion   44
Gecko   46
Tapir   47
Tiny Tales: The Legend of the Pink Dolphin   48

Pygmy Marmoset   50
Tot Lot   52

JUNGLE AND SAVANNA BABIES   54

"The Giraffe"   56
Lion   58
Hippopotamus   59
To the Rescue! The Perfect Pair   60
Gorilla   62
Warthog   64
Dik-dik   65
Baby Buddies: The Odd Couple   66
African Wild Dog   68
Ostrich   69
Tiny Tales: How the Zebra Got Its Stripes   70
Sand Cat   72
Tot Lot   74

DESERT AND COAST BABIES   76

"The Duck and the Kangaroo"   78
Quokka   80
Sugar Glider   81
To the Rescue! Baby Bats Bundle Up   82
Koala   84
Cassowary   86
Platypus   87
Baby Buddies: Orphans Become Pouch Pals   88
Little Penguin   90
Dingo   91
Tiny Tales: How the Kookaburra Got Its Laugh   92
Tasmanian Devil   94
Tot Lot   96

FOREST AND STREAM BABIES

98

"The Eagle (A fragment)"   100
European Hedgehog   102
Brown Hare   103
To the Rescue! Scientists Save Cute Kitties   104
Weasel   106
Alpine Ibex   108
Eurasian Badger   109
Baby Buddies: Sheepdog Becomes Babysitter   110
Red Deer   112
Dormouse   113
Tiny Tales: The Fox and the Crow   114
Tot Lot   116

TROPICS AND PEAKS BABIES

118

"The Rhinoceros"   120
Slow Loris   122
Red Panda   123
To the Rescue! Playtime for Panda Cubs   124
Orangutan   126
Japanese Macaque   128
Indian Paradise Flycatcher   129
Baby Buddies: A Lion, a Tiger, and a Bear—Oh My!   130
Tarsier   132
Yak   133
Tiny Tales: The Legend of the Snow Leopard   134
Tot Lot   136

ICE AND SNOW BABIES

138

"Seal Lullaby"   140
Arctic Fox   142

Reindeer   143
To the Rescue! Scientists Get a Bird's-Eye View   144
Polar Bear   146
Snowy Owl   148
Wolverine   149
Baby Buddies: Seal and Penguin Share a Laugh   150
Arctic Wolf   152
Puffin   153
Tiny Tales: How the Walrus Came to Be   154
Tot Lot   156

OCEAN AND SEA BABIES

158

"We Fish"   160
Clownfish   162
Seahorse   163
Bottlenose Dolphin   164
To the Rescue! Sea Turtles Wear Swimsuits
for Science   166
Pufferfish   168
Octopus   169
Baby Buddies: Sweet Sea Lion Seeks Sidekick   170
Orca   172
Manatee   173
Tiny Tales: Why Whales Don't Live in Lakes   174
Sea Otter   176
Tot Lot   178

"Till To-Morrow."   180
Map of Biomes   182
More on Folktales   184
Index   186
Photo Credits   190
Acknowledgments   192

Introduction

ACROSS THE WORLD, ANIMAL BABIES TAKE TURNS WAKING TO A NEW DAY—AND NEW ADVENTURES!

A kangaroo joey peeks out of its mom's cozy pouch in Australia. A new mustang foal wobbles across dewy North American grass on its long legs. And, at the North Pole, polar bear cubs roll and wrestle in the sparkling snow.

It's time for their parents to get up, too. Some of them are still tired, but their babies won't let them sleep in. A hyena mom yawns as her pups bounce energetically around her. A graceful lioness stretches out in a patch of sunlight, keeping one ear tilted toward her cubs as they practice pouncing. It's time to play!

Whether they're furred, feathered, or anything in between, new babies are a lot of work. And, just like human parents, many animal mommies and daddies spend a lot of time caring for their little ones. Gorillas cradle and cuddle their infants close in their arms. Tiny tarsier moms nestle their babies in the crook of a tree so they can search the forest for food. Coyote fathers hunt while their pups stay safe in the den with their mom. A young spotted snow leopard stays with its mother for as long as two years, copying her every move to learn her survival skills.

Hey, Baby! is filled with the stories of tiny tots that inhabit all corners of the Earth, from the tippy-tops of the Himalaya to the bottom of the deepest seas. You'll get to know them through profiles, poems, folktales, and stories recounting amazing animal rescues and friendships. They're sweet, they're silly, and they're some of the most adorable animal babies on Earth.

Good Morning

The world is hushed in violet hue
and moms are still asleep,
but little paws have set to stir
and chicks begun to cheep.

Little lambs prepare to leap
and robins rustle wing,
as morning rolls across the land
to every feathered thing.

Coyote cubs begin to sing
their verse of morning song,
and waking kittens softly stretch
their toes and fiercely yawn.

Bunnies bound to greet the dawn
where everything is new—
Wake up! It's time to start our day.
There's just so much to do!

—Paige Towler

MOUNTAINS
AND
PLAINS BABIES

The babies of North America

are as different as the landscapes where they live. In the west, brown bear cubs frolic in Alaskan meadows and where the Rocky Mountains stretch their craggy peaks toward the sky. In the central Great Plains, newborn pronghorn take their first shaky steps as grassy fields ripple in the breeze. And on the vast sandy beaches of the Atlantic coast, tiny crabs can be found scurrying along the water's edge where rivers and wetlands empty. From the biggest baby bison to the pudgiest little piglet, here are the tiny tots that leap, crawl, and soar across the United States, Mexico, and Canada.

The Pet Rabbit

"I HAVE a little Bunny with a coat as soft as down,
And nearly all of him is white except one bit of brown.
The first thing in the morning when I get out of bed,
I wonder if my Bunny's still safe in his little shed.

And then the next thing that I do I dare say you have guessed;
It's to go at once and see him, when I am washed and dressed.
And every day I see him I like him more and more,
And each day he is bigger than he was the day before.

I feed him in the morning with bran and bits of bread,
And every night I take some straw to make his little bed.
What with carrots in the morning and turnip-tops for tea,
If a bunny can be happy, I'm sure he ought to be.

Then when it's nearly bedtime I go down to his shed,
And say 'Good night you Bunny' before I go to bed.
I think there's only one thing that would make me happy quite,
If I could take my Bunny dear with me to bed at night?"

—Lizzie Lawson

RABBIT | BABY NAME: Kitten

GROWS UP: In meadows, woodlands, forests, grasslands, deserts, and wetlands across North America

SNACKS ON: Mom's milk, grasses, plants, weeds

PRAIRIE DOG

BABY NAME: Pup

GROWS UP: In North American grasslands

SNACKS ON: Mom's milk, grasses, seeds

The sun rises over the grassland, warming the ground above the prairie dog burrow. It's time for the six-week-old pups to come out and play for the very first time. One by one, the curious pups poke their noses aboveground, whiskers twitching. Soon, they're scampering in the sunshine.

Prairie dogs are very social. They live in groups called prairie dog towns. One town can cover 1,000 acres (405 ha)! Towns are made up of connected underground burrows where dozens of families live. Prairie dog burrows are not too different from human houses: There are nurseries, bedrooms—even bathrooms.

One prairie dog keeps watch over the playing pups. He stands up on his hind legs to see as far as he can. Suddenly, he spots a hawk swooping. He barks to sound the alarm, and all the prairie dogs dive underground to safety. Prairie dogs have a complex language. Their calls can tell others what kind of predator is coming, how big it is, and how fast it's moving. When the hawk flies away, the lookout barks the all-clear signal. It's safe to play outside again!

"I'm related to the squirrels you might have in your backyard."

Massive beasts move slowly across the landscape at Yellowstone National Park in the Northwest United States. Baby calves trot alongside their mothers. Bison are the largest land animals in North America. The males, or bulls, can weigh 2,000 pounds (907 kg)—as much as a small car!

When the calves are born in late spring, their fur is light orange-red. Because of the color, they're sometimes nicknamed "red dogs." After a few months, their dark brown adult hair starts to sprout. Their horns and shoulder humps begin to grow. They're preparing for the winter, when snowfall makes food scarce. In the spring and summer, bison spend up to 11 hours a day eating to gain weight and help them survive the cold months.

Bison have lived in Yellowstone continuously since prehistoric times. During the 19th century, humans hunted almost every last one! But people realized bison needed help and made laws to restrict hunters. Today, thousands of bison once again walk the plains of North America.

BISON

BABY NAME: Calf

GROWS UP: In North American national parks and preserves

SNACKS ON: Mom's milk, grasses, shrubs

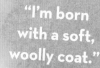

"I'm born with a soft, woolly coat."

BIGHORN SHEEP

BABY NAME: Lamb

GROWS UP: In the Rocky Mountains from southern Canada to northern Mexico

SNACKS ON: Mom's milk, grasses

A baby bighorn sheep stands up for the first time. Born just 15 minutes earlier, the lamb already has a strong instinct to get up and walk. With encouraging nudges from its mother, the baby stretches out one forked hoof and takes a shaky step, and then another. The mother looks on as her brand-new lamb figures out how to use his legs.

Bighorn ewes, or females, give birth to their babies high on cliff ledges where predators can't reach them. It looks dangerous, but bighorn sheep are built for life on the edge. Their hooves are split and have rough bottoms, giving them the ability to grip the rocks.

At one week old, the bighorn lamb prances around, dancing and kicking its feet. It's time to join the herd, a group of five to 15 ewes and their babies. Mother and baby head down the mountain. They hop over boulders and bounce down cliffs, clinging to tiny footholds in the rock. Once with the herd, the lamb spends his days running and jumping with the other lambs. Bighorn sheep are social animals that like to be together.

All that playing is practice for adulthood. The bighorn lamb will grow into a mighty ram. The nubs on his woolly head will become great curling horns, together weighing up to 30 pounds (14 kg), or 10 percent of his entire body weight. A bighorn ram's horns are a status symbol and a weapon. Rams charge toward each other at 20 miles an hour (32 km/h) and smash their horns together. The clash is so loud that it echoes through the mountains!

The fight is mostly for show: Bighorns have a thick, bony skull to protect them from serious injury. Rams will bang their horns together over and over—sometimes for hours—until one gives up. The winner moves toward the herd of ewes. In the coming spring, his own long-legged lamb will take its first steps.

TO THE RESCUE!

BRINGING UP BABY BEARS

The Appalachian Bear Rescue in Townsend, Tennessee, U.S.A., takes in little black bears that are found injured, sick, or orphaned in the nearby Great Smoky Mountains.

The bustling facility has helped more than 250 young bears since it opened in 1996.

In its nursery, curators bottle-feed young cubs every two to three hours and weigh the tiny babies on scales to make sure they're growing. The young bears are moved to an outdoor home as soon as possible, so that they don't learn to depend on humans for survival. At the center's Wild Enclosures, bears learn to run and climb trees—skills they'll need to live on their own. When the bears are strong enough, wildlife officials release them back into the wild.

On June 3, 2016, rescuers released a healthy young black bear named Skipper into the wild. When he arrived at the facility three months

earlier, he had been in bad shape. Veterinarians feared the cub was so weak from not having enough food or water that he might not even survive the night. But thanks to the careful care of his human helpers, Skipper is running free in the mountains between North Carolina and Tennessee.

Helping Hands

Before they set Skipper free, rescuers fitted him with a special accessory: a global positioning system (GPS) tracking collar that collects information about where Skipper goes and how he survives. This information will help people at the Appalachian Bear Rescue figure out the best time and place to release other young bears.

Black bears can also be brown, cinnamon, blue-gray, blue-black, or even (rarely) white.

BEARS LEAVE TOOTH AND CLAW MARKS ON TREES.

THE BEARS ARE WEIGHED TO MAKE SURE THEY ARE GROWING.

THE BEAR FACTS

Black bears are iconic North American animals—the most common bear on the continent. They roam all the way from Canada to Mexico, making their home in forests, mountains, and swamps.

Black bears' favorite activity is eating, and they spend the summer and fall devoted to the task. Like humans, they're omnivores, which means they snack on everything from plants to salmon to small mammals. They have to munch on as much as 18 pounds (8.2 kg) of food each day to stay healthy. That's because they have big bodies to feed: Adult males can weigh as much as 600 pounds (270 kg).

Bears pack on the pounds to prepare for winter, when food is scarce. In the fall, they shelter in caves, cracks in rocks, or under fallen trees. They spend the winter sleeping, living off their body fat. It's during this time that female black bears give birth. Their cubs are born blind and helpless, but by springtime, they're strong enough to emerge from the den with their mother to go searching for food. Bear moms spend the first two years with their babies teaching them how to hunt and survive in the wild. At two, the cubs are all grown up and ready for life on their own!

BEAVER

BABY NAME: Kit

GROWS UP: In waterways of North America

SNACKS ON: Mom's milk, water lily tubers, apples, leaves, bark

A pair of beavers sits together on the banks of a river, gnawing at the base of a willow tree. Using their strong teeth and jaws, the beavers carve away at the tree until it crashes to the forest floor. Beavers are busy creatures. A pair can topple 400 trees in a year!

The beavers work together, carefully interlocking the logs they collect. Beavers are nature's engineers. Using rocks, sticks, and mud, they build a dam that turns a trickling stream into a pond a mile (1.6 km) wide.

On one side of the pond is the beavers' lodge, a house made of branches so strong that even a bear can't break in. The beavers dive underwater and swim through one of the lodge's underwater entrances. Inside, they're raising a family: a litter of six kits.

The beavers will stay with their parents until they're two years old. They learn about building by helping repair the dam. When they're ready, they leave the lodge. It's time to build dams of their own.

MUSTANG

BABY NAME: Foal

GROWS UP: On the grasslands of the western United States

SNACKS ON: Mom's milk, grass, brush

The baby horse leaps across the grassy plain. Her wobbly legs are like skinny toothpicks that seem too long for her body. She stops, balancing on delicate hooves, then wheels around, snorting and kicking. Nearby, her mother grazes, keeping an eye on her playful baby.

The foal is the newest addition to this herd of mustangs living in the grasslands of Wyoming. She's just a few days old, but horses start running almost as soon as they're born. They have to keep up with the herd, which is always moving through the prairie in search of new grass to eat.

North America's mustangs are the descendants of Spanish horses that were brought to the Americas by explorers 500 years ago. Today, mustangs roam across the American West. They live in herds of females, or mares, headed by a lead mare and a male, or stallion. In case of danger, the mare leads the herd to safety and the stallion stays to fight. He wants his foals to grow up strong, into mustangs that will gallop across the grasslands of the West.

BABY BUDDIES

MINI MOUNTAIN LIONS GET SMELLY FRIEND

In the wild, mountain lions and skunks don't get along.

To a mountain lion, a skunk looks like a tasty snack! But that didn't stop these three unlikely animal pals.

Furry Friendship

In 2016, Demetri Price and Meghan Riley of the American wildlife park Animals of Montana had their hands full. They were busy bringing up a newborn skunk named Lilac, who had lost her mother, when another pair of orphans came into their care: baby mountain lion siblings named Riley and Smokey. Suddenly, the keepers were juggling three needy infants!

All three babies had to be bottle-fed every few hours, day and night. So a few weeks in, Price and Riley began putting the babies on the floor together after their feedings. Although skunks are often skittish, Lilac went right up to the little lions. And the curious cats were interested in their new striped friend right away, too. The trio quickly became inseparable.

Adult mountain lions are powerful predators. Sometimes called pumas, cougars, panthers, or cat-amounts, they're the largest wild cats in North America. With their muscular limbs, they can leap as far as 40 feet (12 m)! They usually hunt at night, sneaking up on their target until they're close enough to pounce. They eat both large animals (like deer) and small animals (like skunks). But when mountain lions become friendly with other animals at a young age—like Riley and Smokey did with Lilac the skunk—they can learn to see other creatures as playmates, not prey.

Skunks can spray as far as 10 feet (3 m)!

IT'S PLAYTIME!

STINKY SECURITY

With their striped fur and fluffy tail, skunks may look cute and cuddly. But they have one of the animal kingdom's strongest defense systems. Under the skunk's tail are glands that make an oily liquid. When the skunk feels scared, it turns around and blasts its enemy with a horrible-smelling mist. The stinky spray isn't harmful, but it smells so bad that most predators—even mountain lions—give the skunk plenty of space!

BOBCAT

BABY NAME: Kitten

GROWS UP: In forests, deserts, mountains, and swamps across North America

SNACKS ON: Mom's milk, birds, rodents, bats, deer

"Are we neighbors? I live in almost every state in America."

The sun dips below the horizon. It's nighttime in the forest of Northern California—hunting time for many of the animals that call this place home. The bobcat swivels her large ears as she listens for signs of danger. The coast is clear. Soundlessly, she pads out of her den into the night. Behind her, small cat faces appear. They belong to her six kittens. Tonight, they're going to begin learning to hunt.

There are as many as one million bobcats in the United States. Sometimes called wildcats, bobcats are about twice the size of—and much tougher than—an average house cat. With their long legs and large paws, they are fierce hunters that can bring down adult deer. But most of the time, they eat birds and rodents.

Tonight, the mother bobcat finds a mouse and stands watch as her kittens approach it. They crouch, wiggling their rumps, then pounce. The mouse gets away; the kittens aren't good hunters yet. Before they're ready to live on their own, they'll need more practice!

BALD EAGLE

BABY NAME: Eaglet

GROWS UP: Across most of North America

SNACKS ON: Fish, birds, rodents

High above the ground, near the top of a pine tree in Canada, two bald eagles are building a nest. Partners for life, they work as a team to weave sticks together and create their home. They will keep adding to their nest as long as they live. Some bald eagles' nests grow to nine feet (2.7 m) across and weigh two tons (1.8 t)!

Bald eagles like to build their nests high above the ground. They almost always nest near water, close to the fish that they like to eat. Bald eagles have sharp eyes that can spot fish underwater from high up in the sky.

The eagles will swoop and snag fish with their huge yellow talons. They will bring their catch back to their hungry babies, called eaglets, in the nest. The eagle parents will carefully shred the fish and feed the slivers to their babies. The parents will care for the eaglets, which are born fuzzy instead of feathery, until their adult feathers come in and it's time to fly.

In Latin, the porcupine's name means "quill pig."

PORCUPINE | BABY NAME: Porcupette

GROWS UP: In forests, grasslands, and deserts of North America

SNACKS ON: Mom's milk, leaves, twigs, green plants

Why the Porcupine Has Quills

A LEGEND OF THE OJIBWE NATIVE AMERICAN PEOPLE

Long ago, when the world was first beginning, porcupines had no quills.

One day, Porcupine was out walking through the woods, looking for a plant to eat. Bear came along, wanting to eat him. So Porcupine climbed up high to the top of a tree and was safe there.

The next day, Porcupine was walking through the woods again when he came upon a hawthorn tree. Hawthorn trees are named for their sharp-tipped, thorny branches. When Porcupine walked under the tree, the thorns pricked him. That gave Porcupine an idea. He broke off some of the hawthorn's branches and put them on his back. Then he waited for Bear.

When Bear came along, he sprang on Porcupine, ready to gobble him up. But Porcupine curled himself into a ball. The hawthorn thorns pricked Bear until Bear finally gave up and went away.

Then, a spirit called Nanabozho appeared. He had been watching all along, and he called Porcupine to him and asked, "How did you do that trick?"

"I am always in danger when Bear comes along," said Porcupine. "When I saw those thorns, I thought I would use them to keep myself safe."

Nanabozho thought for a moment. Then, he took some branches from the hawthorn tree and peeled off the bark until they were white. He put some clay on Porcupine's back, stuck the thorns in it, and used magic to make the thorns a part of Porcupine's skin. "Now go into the woods," he told Porcupine.

Porcupine obeyed the spirit. He went into the woods and waited until Wolf came along. Thinking he had spotted a tasty snack, Wolf sprang on Porcupine—but then he ran away howling.

Next, Bear came along, but he saw the thorns and kept away from Porcupine. He was afraid of those thorns! Soon, all the animals learned to stay away from Porcupine. And that is why all porcupines have quills today.

COYOTE

BABY NAME: Pup

GROWS UP: In plains, forests, mountains, and deserts across North America

SNACKS ON: Mom's milk, fruit, insects, frogs, rodents, rabbits, deer

"The best time to hear me howl is at dawn and dusk."

Aaaooooooooooooo!

The haunting howl rings across the desert night. The coyote lowers his snout and takes off, padding silently across the sand. He's on the hunt, looking for a meal to bring back to his five fluffy babies waiting in the den.

Coyotes are solitary creatures that usually like to live alone. But when there are roly-poly pups to care for, the mother and father coyote work as a team. The mother coyote gives birth to her litter in the spring. She can have as many as 12 pups! At first, pups' tiny eyes are closed. Mother coyote stays in the den nursing her babies until their eyes open, at around two weeks old. It's hungry work, and she depends on the father to bring back meals to feed his family.

Outside the safety of the den, the father coyote sniffs the ground. *Rat!* Rats are quick, but the coyote is a master hunter, known for its keen sense of smell and sharp vision. His nose close to the ground, the father coyote tracks the creature through the darkness. Then he spots it, sitting still in the moonlight. The coyote lowers into a crouch. He springs and sprints, racing across the sand at 40 miles an hour (64 km/h). He lunges and—snap!—he catches his prey.

The coyote is hungry. He could gobble up his catch right there. But instead, he turns back toward the den where his hungry family waits. The coyote parents will care for their pups in the den until the little ones are about six months old. By then, the pups will be almost full grown, with adult teeth. It will be time for them to learn the skills they will need to survive on their own. They will leave the den as a family, and the mother coyote will teach them to hunt.

When they're old enough, the coyotes will venture out on their own. On warm summer nights across North America, their young voices will fill the air as they try out their own coyote calls.

Each July, female alligators make nests from mud, plants, and sticks. They lay their eggs and then use more debris to cover them up. When the babies are ready to hatch, she uncovers the nest and sometimes even helps them by gently breaking the shells with her mouth.

Black-footed ferrets were thought to be extinct until 1981, when a ranch dog came home with one in its mouth. Eighteen were captured to raise their young in zoos and wildlife reserves, and their offspring were put out into the wild again. Today, they're making a comeback.

BLACK-FOOTED FERRET

ALLIGATOR

TOT LOT

More little critters from North America's mountains and plains

CHIPMUNK

HUMMINGBIRD

Baby chipmunks are pink, hairless, and born about the size of a jelly bean. Mother chipmunks are very protective of their babies: If one goes missing, she will search for it frantically. After two months, chipmunks are ready to start gathering their own food. They use their cheek pouches like grocery bags to carry as many as 165 acorns in a day!

Hummingbird nests look like a small cup about the size of a walnut shell. The smallest species lay eggs no bigger than a coffee bean. When hummingbird chicks hatch, their eyes are sealed shut and their beaks are no more than a bump. They're so delicate that their predators include large insects!

With its bright green color and the large black dots that resemble eyes on its back, the spicebush swallowtail caterpillar looks just like a green tree snake—a disguise meant to scare off predators. When the caterpillar is ready, it enters a green or brown chrysalis, and then later emerges as a beautiful spicebush swallowtail butterfly.

SPICEBUSH SWALLOWTAIL

OWL

Owl mothers don't build their own nests. Instead, they lay their eggs in the abandoned nests of crows, hawks, or squirrels. The mothers don't care for the eggs alone; father owls sit on the eggs, too, and help care for the chicks when they hatch.

RACCOON

These black-masked bandits start out as cuddly fur balls that live with their mother high in a tree hole. Together, a mother and her baby raccoons are called a nursery.

Newborn opossums are as tiny as honeybees. They crawl into their mother's pouch, where they continue to grow. When they get big enough, they hop in and out of the pouch and sometimes even ride on their mother's back as she looks for food.

OPOSSUM

RIVER AND RAIN FOREST BABIES

The babies of South America

get their nourishment from the mighty Amazon River. The largest river in the world, the Amazon winds down the continent like a giant snake and feeds the lush, green rain forest. There are more kinds of plants and animals in the Amazon rain forest than there are anywhere else on Earth! Riding on their parents' backs, newborn spider monkeys leap from tree to tree. Baby sloths hang with their moms. Tiny geckos cling to twigs. Ocelot kittens scamper through the shadows. From the tip-tops of the trees to the tiniest pools of water, South America is where these babies make their home.

Frog Ballet

Socks the shade of orange zest,
a lime waistcoat, a snowy vest,
the only clothes I need to prance
from leaf to leaf and plant to plant.

My legs cast an electric hue
of dancer's tights in cobalt blue.
I whirl, I twirl, I seem to fly,
a dashing flash of ruby eye

commanding the rain forest stage—
the best you've ever seen, I'd wage.
And though I'm small, I'll have you know:
It's no surprise—I steal the show!

—Paige Towler

FROG | BABY NAME: Tadpole

GROWS UP: In the tropical forests from Costa Rica to Brazil

SNACKS ON: Flies, ants, insects, spiders, termites

Frogs hatch from their eggs as swimming tadpoles, then grow legs and transform into their adult forms.

TAMANDUA

A tamandua moves slowly through the treetops, using her curving claws to grasp the branches. She's not alone: On her back, her baby is hanging on for the ride!

Tamanduas spend most of their days snoozing in hollow tree trunks. At night, it's time to hunt. Tamanduas have small eyes and can't see very well. But their long nose makes them great at sniffing out their favorite snacks: termites and ants. When a tamandua finds an insect nest, it will dig a hole to reach it. Then, using its 16-inch (41 cm)-long sticky tongue, it slurps up its prey. A tamandua can eat almost 9,000 ants in a single day!

Tamanduas have just one baby at a time. While young, they spend their time riding piggyback on their mothers and learning how to hunt. Soon, they'll be experts: Amazonian Indians sometimes use tamanduas to keep their homes insect free!

On a fallen tree branch bridging a rain forest stream, a mother ocelot stands as still as a statue. Her spotted kitten crouches beside her, watching her mother's every move. Suddenly, the mother ocelot strikes at the water with a speedy paw and flips a flopping fish onto the stream bank. She's teaching her kitten how to hunt.

Ocelots are one of South America's most mysterious animals. These small cats, twice the size of a house cat, spend the day sleeping. They snooze in bushes, on a branch, or inside a hollow tree. At night ocelots wake up to prowl. They move almost silently through the dense forests where they live.

These stealthy hunters have very good vision and hearing. Their eyes are specially adapted for night hunting; these special eyes help the ocelot see as well at night as a human can during the day. Like house cats, ocelots are good climbers and jumpers. But, unlike house cats, they're also good swimmers that love the water!

OCELOT

BABY NAME: Kitten

GROWS UP: In the South American rain forest, but can be found as far north as Texas

SNACKS ON: Mom's milk, rabbits, rodents, iguanas, fish, frogs

"I'm born with blue eyes that will turn brown when I grow up."

TO THE RESCUE!

SAVING SLOTHS

Sloths have mouths shaped into permanent smiles and love nothing more than a nice, long nap.

So it might seem as if these adorable animals don't have a care in the world. But sloths do face dangers—when humans move into their South American rain forests. Sometimes, orphaned sloths are left without mothers to care for them. That's where the Sloth Institute comes in. This organization in Manuel Antonio, Costa Rica, raises orphaned baby sloths and releases them back into the wild.

Born to Be Wild

In 2013, Sam Trull moved to Costa Rica and met Kermie, a two-week-old baby sloth that had recently lost his mother. Trull fell in love with the tiny, round-eyed baby. She cuddled him, fed him, and played with him. All the while, she hoped to someday release the little sloth back into his jungle home. In 2014, she founded the Sloth Institute to help rehabilitate Kermie and other orphaned sloths so they could once again live free.

But Trull found that getting sloths ready to live on their own isn't so easy. Because baby sloths learn survival skills from their mothers, Kermie didn't know the first thing about life in the jungle. Trull and her team couldn't simply set him free, because he wouldn't survive. Instead, they use a method called a "soft release," a way of getting a captive animal slowly used to its natural habitat.

In 2015, Trull and her team decided Kermie was ready to begin the process. First, they set up a large cage in the jungle for Kermie and Ellen, another sloth who came to the center as a baby. Once the sloths became familiar with their wild surroundings, the team opened the cage door. The sloths could come and go as they pleased, venturing out into the jungle, and then returning to the safety of their cage until they felt ready to live totally on their own. Today, Kermie and Ellen live wild and free—as they were born to be.

KERMIE LIKES HIS HAMMOCK.

Sloths in captivity sleep for 15 to 20 hours a day.

CUDDLE TIME!

LIFE AT SLOTH SPEED

Sloths spend almost their whole lives in trees. They even give birth up there, far above the rain forest floor! Sloths have one baby at a time, and the mother and her infant have a close bond. The baby catches a ride through the rain forest by clinging to his mother's belly for several weeks after birth. Even once they're too big to ride, young sloths stay close by their mothers for up to four years.

Sloths are famous for their slow-motion way of moving. But the animals aren't lazy: They don't get much energy from their leafy diet. The tough leaves are difficult to digest. Sloths have four stomachs to do the job, but it can still take a month for them to digest one meal. That explains why sloths are so slow!

39

GUANACO

BABY NAME: Chulengo

GROWS UP: In the mountains, plateaus, and plains of South America

SNACKS ON: Mom's milk, grass, leaves, shoots

South America is home to the Andes mountains—and to the baby guanacos born on their windy hilltops. A newborn's mother licks his fur clean, and it dries into a soft, fluffy coat. Within five minutes after his birth, the baby stands up, ready to follow his mother through the winding mountain trails.

Guanacos are smaller, wild relatives of the camel. Unlike camels, guanacos don't have humps on their backs. But their feet are very similar to a camel's, with two squishy, padded toes on each foot that help them grip rocky trails. These feet are ideal for living in the Andes mountains as high as 13,000 feet (3,962 m) above sea level. Up here, oxygen is scarce, making it hard for most animals to run and jump. But guanacos have special blood that can carry extra oxygen to help them survive in their hilltop habitats. Even though they're smaller than horses, guanacos can run just as fast—up to 40 miles an hour (64 km/h)!

As the largest plant eaters in South America's dry lands, guanacos can't afford to be picky about their diets. They like to eat grasses and shrubs, but when those aren't available, they'll even eat succulents and cacti! Their stomachs have three chambers, which help them get the most nutrients out of those tough plants.

Like many other animals, guanacos communicate with each other by positioning their ears, body, and tail. They also make lots of different noises, from high-pitched squeals to snorts to alarm calls that sound a little like they're laughing. Strangest of all, guanacos sometimes spit to get their point across. They can shoot a mouthful of grass as far as six feet (1.8 m)—and they have great aim! So although these mountain dwellers are usually shy and gentle, if you meet one in the wild, make sure to stay on its good side!

Guanacos live in herds of up to 50.

ARMADILLO

BABY NAME: Pup

GROWS UP: In prairies, savannas, and wetlands across Central and South America and as far north as the southern United States

SNACKS ON: Mom's milk, insects, larvae

Twelve armadillo pups are curled up underground in their burrow. Even though they're just newborns, they look like miniature adults. Their mother will nurse them for two to four months before they can begin hunting for insects to munch on.

Armadillos spend the early mornings and evenings looking for beetles, ants, termites, and other insects to eat. They don't have good eyesight, but they use their sensitive nose to sniff out these tasty treats. And if the meal they want is underground, they'll use their long front claws to dig it up. When they're not eating, armadillos love to nap: They can spend 16 hours a day sleeping in their burrows!

In Spanish, the armadillo's name means "little armored one." Bony plates cover the back, head, legs, and tail of most of these strange-looking creatures. Armadillos are related to anteaters and sloths. But they're the only mammals alive today that wear these shells.

A baby capybara has gotten separated from her mother. Distressed, she lets out a series of purrs and whistles. Her mom comes running to find her. Capybaras are vocal animals that use noises to keep in touch while they're grazing. They can bark, huff, growl, and even whinny.

Capybaras are the largest rodents in the world, standing up to two feet (0.6 m) tall. Though they are closely related to guinea pigs, capybaras have much more in common with a totally different animal: the hippopotamus! Like hippos, capybaras are good swimmers that like to hide in the water, with just their eyes, ears, and nostrils sticking out above the surface. They can even dive down and stay underwater for up to five minutes at a time.

Capybaras have long, sharp teeth that are good for grazing on grass and water plants. Their two long front teeth never stop growing! They're worn down by constant chewing—adult capybaras can eat eight pounds (3.6 kg) in a day! Baby capybaras start grazing when they're only a few days old.

CAPYBARA

BABY NAME: Pup

GROWS UP: Swampy, grassy regions of Central and South America

SNACKS ON: Mom's milk, grass, water plants, reeds

BABY BUDDIES

MINI MONKEY GETS CUDDLY COMPANION

In the wild, mother spider monkeys carry their babies with them wherever they go.

But baby Estela was abandoned when she was born, leaving the tiny primate all alone. Like many creatures, Estela needed a companion. And when a real-life monkey wasn't an option, her keepers got creative: They gave the little critter a stuffed monkey to cuddle up to!

Plush Primate

At the Melbourne Zoo in Australia, keepers who were raising the little monkey feared that without her mother's caring touch, baby Estela might not grow up into a normal, healthy monkey. But if her human caregivers stepped into the parenting role, Estela would lose the natural fear of people that would later keep her safe in the wild. The plush parent was their smart solution to the problem.

Baby Estela took to her cuddly companion right away. She clung to the stuffed monkey just as she would have held tightly to her real mother. Estela even took naps on the back of another plush partner: a stuffed kitty. The tiny tot's toy companions helped the little spider monkey feel loved and safe.

All the while, zookeepers kept careful watch over baby Estela, who was fragile and sick when she was first born. They held her, fed her, and even took turns sleeping next to her—but they were always careful that Estela didn't get too used to human contact. Under their watchful eye, the little monkey began to grow stronger.

Once Estela was healthy enough, her keepers introduced her to Sonja, her grandmother. The keepers had high hopes that Sonja would be a good monkey role model, and they were thrilled when Sonja showed interest in Estela right away. The older monkey began to teach her young granddaughter all about being a spider monkey: how to climb trees, find fruit, and get along with other monkeys. Estela learned fast, and the pair made their debut at the zoo's primate nursery when the baby spider monkey turned four months old.

44

FRIENDS FOREVER

Spider monkeys got their names for their long, thin limbs and tails, which make them look a little like spiders.

FEEDING TIME

ESTELA AND GRANDMA

LIFE IN THE TREETOPS

In the wild, spider monkeys use their long, thin arms to swing through the trees. They even use their special tail like a fifth limb: They grasp tree branches with it just like a hand! Spider monkeys spend their days searching for fruit in the trees, where they live. They love the companionship of other monkeys, living in groups of up to 100. The monkeys will wrap their tails around each other and even give hugs!

Adult spider monkeys are dark brown, but their babies are born with a pink face and ears. Females usually give birth to just one baby at a time, which is carried on its mother's stomach until it's about four months old. Then, the baby is strong enough to switch to riding on its mother's back. This constant companionship allows baby spider monkeys to learn all the skills they'll need to survive on their own.

A mother gecko lays her eggs under tree bark on the forest floor and then leaves her babies in the hands of fate. The temperature of the air determines the new geckos' gender: If it's around 80°F (26.7°C) while the eggs incubate, the hatchlings will be females. At 90°F (32.2°C), they'll be males.

Most geckos don't have blinking eyelids, so they use their long tongue to keep their eyes clean. That's just one of their odd traits. Experts also believe geckos are the only lizards on Earth that call to each other. Depending on the species, they might squeak, croak, hiss—or even roar!

Geckos have abilities so amazing they almost seem like superpowers. Whereas humans and most other animals are color-blind at night, geckos can see colors using just the light of the moon. If a predator catches them, they can instantly shed their tails, which wiggle around and distract the enemy until the gecko can get away. The little lizard then simply grows a new tail. And, using their unique gripping feet, geckos can walk up walls and even upside down along ceilings.

GECKO

BABY NAME: Hatchling

GROWS UP: In warm climates throughout the world

SNACKS ON: Insects

TAPIR

BABY NAME: Calf

GROWS UP: In the swamps, forests, savanna, and rain forests of Central and South America and as far north as Mexico

SNACKS ON: Mom's milk, leaves, fruit, grasses

The baby tapir is curled up on the forest floor. If you didn't know she was there, you'd have a hard time spotting her. Her brown-and-beige stripes help her blend in perfectly with her surroundings.

Tapirs look like they're related to pigs or anteaters, but they're actually a separate species. The tapir's unusual nose is a flexible trunk that the creature uses to sniff out food and rip leaves off branches—and even as a snorkel when the animal is underwater! Tapirs love to cool off in lakes, rivers, and ponds. They learn to swim when they're just a few days old.

To find their watering holes, tapirs follow winding trails made by the feet of many tapirs traveling the same path over time. They snack on all kinds of plants—and along with them, the plants' seeds. As they roam, the tapirs poop out the seeds, spreading them throughout the forest and planting the next generation of vegetation. Tapirs have performed this role as farmers of the forest for millions of years.

47

DOLPHIN

BABY NAME: Calf

GROWS UP: Throughout much of South America's Amazon and Orinoco River basins

SNACKS ON: Mom's milk, piranhas and other fish, shrimps, crabs, turtles

"My pink color brightens when I get excited or surprised."

The Legend of the Pink Dolphin

ADAPTED FROM A BRAZILIAN FOLKTALE

When the wet season arrives in South America each year, the vast Amazon River overflows its banks. The rain forest floods. Fish and frogs paddle around underwater trees and plants. And with them swim the Amazon dolphins. As pink as bubble gum, these freshwater dolphins are found nowhere else on Earth. For thousands of years, they've lived side by side with the people of the Amazon, who call them *botos*.

Legend has it that beneath the Amazon's surface is a fairyland called Encante, where the enchanted botos live. Long ago, the botos were humans, and still today, each one has the ability to turn back into a person whenever it wants to. Most of the time, the botos are content with their magnificent lives beneath the waves. But sometimes, one will come ashore and shape-shift into its human form to walk among the people once again.

When a boto comes ashore, it always appears as a well-dressed man. He wears a stylish suit of purest white and walks down the street to the nearest party. There, he dances. He dances so well it is as if he has always had two legs instead of a dolphin's tail. Enamored with his beauty and grace, a woman at the party will fall instantly in love with him. But at the end of the night, her new sweetheart will disappear. He has gone back to the river and become a dolphin once again.

The botos are powerful creatures to be honored, but they are feared, too. With their magical powers, they can enchant humans and take them down below the river's surface to Encante, never to return. Even today, some Amazonians don't go near the river waters at dawn and dusk—the time when the botos make their mischief.

The stories say that there is only one way to find out whether a person is a boto or merely a man in a white suit. When a boto comes ashore and assumes the look of a human, it wears a hat on its head to cover its dolphin blowhole. Find a way to trick the suit-wearer into taking off his hat and you'll know once and for all whether he's a man—or one of the Amazon's enchanted pink dolphins.

"Our whole family helps raise us."

PYGMY MARMOSET

BABY NAME: Infant

GROWS UP: In the forests of Brazil, Colombia, Peru, Ecuador, and Bolivia

SNACKS ON: Mom's milk, sap, insects, nectar, fruit

High in the canopy of the rain forest, a tiny creature dashes through the trees. It ducks behind trunks and branches, freezes, then leaps to the next tree. Then, more of the animals appear: It's a family of miniature monkeys!

Pygmy marmosets are one of the smallest monkey species on the planet. Once full grown, they weigh no more than a stick of butter and average just 5.35 inches (13.6 cm) long. Their small size is a big advantage in the rain forests where they live; it allows them to cling to twigs far too tiny to support most animals. The monkeys are expert tree climbers and will fling themselves through the treetops like acrobats.

Pygmy marmosets are so good at tree climbing because that's how they get to their favorite food: tree sap. Using their sharp lower teeth, they scrape a hole in a vine or bark. When sap begins to flow into the hole, they lick it up with their tongue. This work keeps pygmy marmosets busy: They've been known to make up to 1,300 holes in their favorite trees!

Marmoset mothers almost always give birth to twins. The newborns are about the size of a human thumb! Pygmy marmosets live in close family groups of a pair of monkeys, their adult children, and their babies. Everyone takes care of the babies. The father helps deliver his children, cleans them up, and carries the newborns piggyback for their first two weeks of life, bringing them back to their mother whenever it's time to nurse.

Once they're a few months old, the group's youngest members are ready to forage for food with the rest of the troop. They'll spend the rest of their lives with their families, hopping from tree to tree in the South American forest.

Agoutis have waterproof coats and ears so sensitive that they can hear when fruit—their favorite food—falls from a tree and hits the forest floor. When these romantic rodents find another agouti they like, they mate for life and raise their babies in a nest of leaves, roots, and hair.

AGOUTI

OLINGUITO

This animal, which looks like a cross between a cat and a teddy bear, wasn't discovered until 2013. Not much is yet known about this mysterious creature, which lives high in the cloud forests of Colombia and Ecuador.

TOT LOT

More itty-bitty babies from the rivers and rain forests of South America

TOUCAN

Toucans are best known for their bills, which can be nearly as long as the rest of their bodies. Scientists aren't sure why they have such a big bill: It might help them scare away predators, attract mates, or reach food hanging at the tips of branches. Toucan parents both sit on the eggs and bring their newly hatched babies food to eat.

GALÁPAGOS TORTOISE

When these tortoises are born in their nests under the sand, they first have to crack open their shells and climb out. Then they must dig their way to the surface—which might take the tiny tortoises a month! These reptiles don't stay small for long; they grow to giants that can weigh more than 500 pounds (227 kg).

COATI

This raccoon relative uses its long, flexible nose to investigate small gaps between rocks and underneath piles of leaves. It's looking for tasty grubs, or beetle larvae. Coatis are chatty creatures that click, grunt, whistle, and bark as they search for food.

Chinchillas are native to the Andes mountains of northern Chile, but they're often kept as pets. Newborn chinchillas weigh only 1.2 ounces (35 g). Born fully furred and with their eyes open, they look like tiny versions of their parents.

CHINCHILLA

BLUE-FOOTED BOOBY

These birds love to show off their brightly colored feet; males strut around would-be mates, stepping high to put them in full view. To females, the bluer the feet, the handsomer the male booby! These vibrant toes perform double duty: Boobies also use them to cover their young and keep them warm.

ANDEAN BEAR

The Andean bear is also known as the spectacled bear because of the rings of light fur around its eyes. These bears are so shy that very little is known about them. When a mother bear emerges from her den with her baby, she'll carry the little bear on her back or clutched to her chest with one front paw.

JUNGLE AND SAVANNA BABIES

A herd of giraffes moves across the African landscape, where grasses wave as far as the eye can see. Calves totter on long legs, staying close to mom's side. A pair of mighty lions watches lazily, their cubs rolling and wrestling nearby. Beyond the savannas of Africa, there are vast deserts, tall mountains, and tropical jungles. All kinds of amazing animals make this land their home, from bouncing baby baboons to snuggly small sand cats. These are the babies that toddle, pounce, and wrestle from Morocco to Madagascar.

The Giraffe

My neck is long,
I know it's true.
I do enjoy my special view
of savanna plains and scattered trees,
of elephants munching on grass and leaves,
of zebras, birds, and buffalo,
of sky above and bugs below.
But, oh, how I wish from this day on
I could be as tall as my mom!

—Jen Agresta

GIRAFFE | BABY NAME: Calf

GROWS UP: In pockets of Africa south of the Sahara

SNACKS ON: Mom's milk, leaves

57

LION

BABY NAME: Cub

GROWS UP: In the grasslands of Africa

SNACKS ON: Mom's milk, mice, rabbits, antelope, zebras

The newborn lion cubs wait quietly in their hiding spot in a clump of grasses. The mother lioness keeps them hidden there to protect them from predators, visiting her mewing babies only to feed them.

When the cubs are six weeks old, the mother decides it's time to introduce them to the pride, or lion family. A pride is made up of a few male lions and a dozen females that are mothers, sisters, and cousins to each other. Female lions do most of the hunting for the pride. They form hunting parties that work as a team to corner speedy animals like antelope and zebras.

The lionesses in a pride often give birth around the same time. That means their cubs have lots of playmates! When the female cubs grow up, they may stay with the pride their whole lives. Male lions will leave to find prides of their own. They'll use their mighty roars—which can carry as far as five miles (8 km)—to warn predators to stay away and to keep their families safe.

A **hippopotamus mother and her baby** bask on the river shoreline. Their ears wiggle as they wallow in the muddy water, where they spend most of every day. Hippos love water: That's why, upon spotting the animals in Africa, the ancient Greeks gave them their name, which means "water horse" or "river horse."

Hippos spend up to 16 hours a day in the water, with just the tops of their ears and noses peeking above the surface. Lazing in the cool water keeps their big bodies from overheating in the blazing African sun. Hippos can't swim, so they push off the bottom of the river in a slow-motion gallop. They can dunk and hold their breath for as long as five minutes. They can even sleep underwater, bobbing up to take a breath and sinking back down to the bottom without waking up!

Baby hippos close their ears and nostrils so they can nurse from their mothers underwater. After eight months, they've grown strong enough to leave the safety of the river, staying close by their mother's side while she grazes during the night. Hippo calves may be cute, but they grow up to be one of Africa's most ferocious animals. These chubby critters may not look it, but they can unleash a mighty fury on any predator that gets too close for comfort.

HIPPOPOTAMUS

BABY NAME: Calf

GROWS UP: In slow-moving rivers and lakes across Africa

SNACKS ON: Mom's milk, grass

"I'll grow up to be the third largest land animal in the world."

TO THE RESCUE!

THE PERFECT PAIR

In 2014, two orphaned baby elephants were discovered in the wild.

One, later named Kamok, was just one day old when her mother abandoned her. Weak and hungry, Kamok wandered into a camp on Kenya's Ol Pejeta Conservancy, where rangers began bottle-feeding her. Two months later, rangers at the nearby Kenya Wildlife Service Manyani Ranger Training Academy were awoken in the night by frightened screams. They followed the sound to a deep, drying water hole. Stuck at the bottom, there was another baby: a scared and lonely three-week-old calf later named Ashaka.

Pachyderm Pals

Baby elephants need expert care to grow up into big, strong adults. So the rangers brought Kamok and Ashaka to the David Sheldrick Wildlife Trust, a rescue center outside Nairobi, Kenya, that has lots of experience raising infant elephants. There, the two calves met and became instant friends. The babies spent their days side by side, running through the grass and rolling around in the mud.

The David Sheldrick Wildlife Trust takes in orphaned elephants like Kamok and Ashaka and raises them for as long as two years, until they don't depend on milk anymore. Hand-raising little elephants is a big job: Rangers at the center give the babies cooling mud baths and feed them with giant bottles. Over the past 40 years, they have successfully raised more than 150 infant elephants!

Once the young elephants are strong enough, they're moved to two centers in Tsavo National Park, where they are gradually reintroduced into the wild. That can take as long as 10 years! When the babies are ready, they are released back into the forest, where they'll go on to nurture wild elephant babies of their own.

ELEPHANTS ARE SOCIAL ANIMALS.

ASHAKA AND KAMOK

FAMILY TIES

Kamok and Ashaka's friendship was more than just adorable to watch: The babies' bond was important for keeping them happy and healthy. In the wild, elephants form close ties with their family members. In fact, all the females in an elephant family pitch in to care for new calves: mothers, sisters, cousins, aunts, grandmothers, and family friends. When a calf feels scared, all the other elephants comfort and protect it. These relationships last for the elephant's entire life—as long as 70 years. Sometimes, an elephant will leave the family to join a new herd. But even then, they'll keep in touch with rumbling calls that can be heard far across the savanna.

GORILLA

BABY NAME: Infant

GROWS UP: In Africa's rain forests

SNACKS ON: Mom's milk, leaves, fruits, seeds, roots, ants, termites

"When I'm first born, I weigh about four pounds (2 kg)."

The mother gorilla sits on the ground, using one hand to hold a piece of fruit she's munching on. Cradled in her other arm is her newborn baby. Baby gorillas are called infants, just like human babies. And they're similar to humans in lots of other ways, too.

Young gorillas wrestle and play tag and follow the leader. They learn by imitating other members in their family group, called a troop. All the adult gorillas are gentle with the infants—even the massive silverback, the smart and strong male leader of the troop. The silverback keeps his troop of five to 30 gorillas safe and makes all their decisions, including when they will rest, when they will eat, and where they will spend the night.

After mornings spent snacking on leaves, seeds, and the occasional insect, the gorilla troop turns in for a midday nap. Each adult gorilla gathers leaves and branches and constructs a nest. Then they take a snooze while the young gorillas play. After naptime, the gorillas eat again until it's time for bed, when they build another nest to spend the night in. Young gorillas sleep with their mothers until they learn to make their own nests. Nest-building is a tough skill—it takes gorillas between four and six years to master it!

Many people think gorillas are ferocious, aggressive creatures. And when silverbacks sense a threat to their troop, they will beat their chests, scream, bare their teeth, and charge. It's enough to make anybody turn and run! But even though they look scary, gorillas are really gentle giants that prefer to spend their days munching on plants and romping with their families.

"My tusks will grow to be up to two feet (0.6 m) long!"

WARTHOG

BABY NAME: Piglet

GROWS UP: In Africa's woodlands and grasslands

SNACKS ON: Mom's milk, plants, roots

When it comes time for a warthog female, or sow, to give birth, she lines a burrow with leaves and grasses. She usually has two or three baby piglets. The fuzzy newborns don't have warts or tusks yet. Those will come in later, as the little warthogs grow up into one of Africa's most oddball animals!

An adult male warthog has a large, flat head covered with "warts"—actually bumps that help protect his face during fights with other males. He's mostly bald except for a few tufts of hair. And he has four sharp tusks. Although they look ferocious, warthogs are grazers that like to snack on grasses and plants, and they use their snouts to dig for roots. When faced with danger, warthogs would rather run than stand and fight. They can reach speeds of 30 miles an hour (48 km/h)—faster than the fastest human sprinters!

When it's too hot or too cold aboveground, warthogs like to stay cozy in their burrows underground. They don't dig their own burrows: Instead, they find natural holes or take over those abandoned by aardvarks.

A **dik-dik stands at attention in the grass.** She's just seen a hungry hyena, and she's on high alert. "Dik-dik! Dik-dik!" she whistles. Then she takes off, running a zigzag pattern through the grass that's meant to throw off the predator.

Dik-diks are named for the sound of their alarm calls. These small antelope stand just over a foot (0.3 m) high at the shoulder. If their snouts look a little strange, it's because they're more than just noses: They're built-in air conditioners that keep dik-diks from overheating, even when temperatures reach 104°F (40°C).

Although most antelope live in herds, dik-diks spend their whole lives with just their partners. They have only one baby at a time, which stays with the parents until the next baby is born. Then, it's time for a new adventure—to grow up and go have a family of its own!

DIK-DIK

BABY NAME: Fawn

GROWS UP: In the grasslands of eastern and southwestern Africa

SNACKS ON: Mom's milk, shrubs, leaves, fruit, berries

BABY BUDDIES

THE ODD COUPLE

In 2011, zookeepers at Busch Gardens in Tampa, Florida, were put in charge of caring for a three-week-old orphaned cheetah.

They bottle-fed the furry newborn around the clock. But they knew that he needed something else: friendship. So they set out to find another rescue animal to be the cub's companion: a Labrador retriever puppy from a local animal shelter.

Wild About You

The six-week-old puppy was smart, playful, and patient—all traits the zookeepers thought might make her a good friend. And they were right. When the puppy met the cheetah cub, they became buddies right away. Busch Gardens staff held an online vote to name the interspecies pals. The cheetah was called Kasi, Swahili for "one with speed," and the pup was named Mtani, meaning "close friend."

Mtani the puppy lived up to her name. With her friendly personality, she encouraged Kasi the cheetah to romp and play better than a human caregiver could have. And even though the cheetah would

grow up faster and stronger, Mtani became top dog in the relationship: Kasi let the pup win when they wrestled!

When Kasi and Mtani were young, they spent almost all of their time together. They played chase in Kasi's grassy enclosure. When they got tired, they napped in the sunshine together. And people flocked to see the unusual dog-and-cheetah duo.

The pair remained fast friends until they were two years old. By then, the animals weren't babies anymore. Zookeepers noticed that Kasi had started to become interested in the female cheetahs in the enclosure next to his. They introduced Kasi to a female named Jenna, and the two cheetahs bonded, just as they would in the grasslands of their African home. As for Mtani, the dog went to live with one of the Busch Gardens staff members. Her mission accomplished, she traded running with Earth's fastest mammal for snoozing on the couch.

BORN TO RUN

The fastest land animal on Earth, the cheetah can accelerate from 0 to 60 miles an hour (96 km/h) in only three seconds—much faster than most cars! Cheetahs are the sprinters of the animal world, with bodies designed to run very fast for short distances. They have a flexible spine that gives their front legs maximum reach forward on each stride. They have claws that grip the ground like sports cleats. And their oversize nostrils, lungs, and heart help them push themselves for extreme speed. These fleet felines are so fast that they can chase down some of Africa's speediest runners, like gazelles, wildebeest, and impalas. A cheetah's chase takes so much energy that it needs a half hour to catch its breath before it's ready to eat!

FAITHFUL FRIENDS KASI AND MTANI

The dark marks that run from the inner corner of a cheetah's eyes to its mouth help reflect the glare of the bright African sun.

"Most dogs have five toes on each foot, but I have only four."

The **African wild dog walks** amid his litter of puppies. Sometimes called the painted dog, his coat is a beautiful watercolor of browns, blacks, and whites. He nuzzles the babies as he goes, wagging his tail. His puppies are the newest additions to the family, or pack, that lives on the savanna.

When African wild dog puppies reach about four weeks of age, it's time for them to graduate from milk to meat. All the members of the pack take turns feeding the pups by eating and then regurgitating their food so that it's soft and easy to chew. This may sound gross to humans, but it's how many animals feed their babies!

When the puppies are about three months old, they're strong enough to follow the adults on a hunt. There's a lot puppies need to learn: African wild dogs use teamwork to take down large animals like antelope. They communicate with high-pitched squeaking sounds and point with their large ears to show which direction to go or what to do. Once they learn the ropes, the pups will grow up to be smart and savvy hunters.

AFRICAN WILD DOG

BABY NAME: Puppy

GROWS UP: In the open woodlands, grasslands, and savannas of southern Africa and southern East Africa

SNACKS ON: Mom's milk, antelope, wildebeest, rodents, birds

OSTRICH

BABY NAME: Chick

GROWS UP: In the savanna, desert, and open woodlands of central and southern Africa

SNACKS ON: Plants, roots, fruit, insects, lizards, small rodents

The baby ostrich is hatching out of her egg. As she pecks with her beak and pushes with her feet, her mother swoops in to help out, gently cracking the shell so her baby can hatch.

Ostriches are the world's largest bird, standing eight feet (2.5 m) when fully grown. They're too big to fly, but ostriches are strong, speedy runners. With their muscular legs, they can sprint up to 43 miles an hour (70 km/h). And their wings aren't useless: Ostriches use them to help them turn when they're running at top speed.

Ostriches live in small herds of fewer than a dozen birds with one dominant female, or hen. All the females in the group will place their eggs in her nest. Then, both the dominant hen and the herd's dominant male take turns sitting on the eggs until they're ready to hatch. Each enormous egg weighs as much as two dozen chicken eggs!

No two zebras have the same stripe pattern.

ZEBRA | BABY NAME: Foal

GROWS UP: In grasslands, savannas, woodlands, scrublands, and hills across Africa

SNACKS ON: Mom's milk, grasses, shrubs, leaves, bark, twigs

How the Zebra Got Its Stripes

ADAPTED FROM A LEGEND OF THE SAN PEOPLE OF THE KALAHARI DESERT

Long ago, when animals were still new to the Earth, the weather was very hot. There wasn't much water, and there were only a few pools in Africa.

One of these pools was guarded by an unruly baboon. He claimed to be the lord of the water, and he forbade any of the other animals from drinking from his pool.

One fine day, a zebra came to the pool to have a drink of water. In those days, zebras had pure white fur. The baboon, who was sitting by his fire next to the water hole, leaped up and yelled, "Go away! This is my pool and I am the lord of the water!"

The zebra shouted back, "The water is for everyone, not just for you, you mean old monkey!"

"If you want water, you'll have to fight me for it!" said the baboon. The zebra leaped at the baboon, and the two began to battle.

Back and forth they went, sending a huge cloud of dust into the sky. Then, with a mighty kick, the zebra sent the baboon flying high up on the cliff. The baboon landed with a smack on his seat, scraping all the hair clean off. To this day, the baboon still has a bare patch where he landed.

Tired, the zebra stumbled backward into the baboon's fire. The flames scorched him, burning black stripes into his white fur. Shocked, the zebra went galloping away to the savanna. He's been there ever since, and his fur is striped to this day.

SAND CAT

BABY NAME: Kitten

GROWS UP: In the deserts of North Africa and the Middle East

SNACKS ON: Mom's milk, rodents, birds, reptiles, snakes

"When full grown, I can sprint at speeds up to 25 miles an hour (40 km/h)."

The wild cat sits outside of her rock burrow. With her big eyes, fluffy ears, and small nose, this adorable six-pound (2.7-kg) cat looks like a kitten. But she's an adult sand cat, one of the smallest wild cats in the world.

Sand cats are the only kind of cat that makes the desert their primary home. They are built to handle the dry, sandy conditions and survive temperatures as high as 126°F (52°C). Their huge ears release heat, helping them keep cool, and they have thick black fur on the bottom of their feet to protect them from the hot desert sand. Amazingly, they don't ever need to drink water: Sand cats get all they need from their food.

Sand cats do their hunting at night when it's coolest. They use their large ears to sense prey underground, and then they dig to reach it. Sand cats are ferocious hunters that will even battle poisonous snakes, like the horned sand viper. But the cats have a soft side, too—they meow to get attention and purr when they're content, just like house cats.

During the heat of the day, they stay inside their burrows, which they take over from foxes, porcupines, or rodents. Burrows are also where mother sand cats raise their babies; they usually have between three and five kittens at a time. Because sand cats are solitary animals that spend most of their lives alone, the kittens will leave home to find their own territories at as young as three or four months old.

Because they live in remote, extreme environments, sand cats are hard for scientists to study. That means that many things about them are still a mystery. One thing is for sure: They're one of Africa's most adorable animals.

CHIMPANZEE

Baby chimps cling to their mother's back, piggyback style, and hang on tight as she swings through the trees. The infants stay with their mothers until they're seven years old, and just like humans, they may develop bonds that last a lifetime.

AFRICAN CIVET

Civets have special scent glands that produce a musky odor. In the wild, civets use this strong smell to mark their territories, but some people prize it as a perfume ingredient!

TOT LOT

More tiny tykes from the jungles and savannas of Africa

OKAPI

Okapi communicate with calls of such low frequency that humans can't hear them. Scientists think mother okapis may use these calls to make sure their calves are okay while they're out grazing. Because the calls are so low-pitched, an okapi can talk to her baby without predators listening in!

GUNDI

These guinea pig-like creatures live in the rocky deserts of northern Africa. Because water is so scarce there, mother gundis produce very little milk, and their babies eat solid food within four weeks.

FENNEC FOX

This fox, the world's smallest, has oversize ears that help cool this desert dweller. Fennec foxes mate for life, and both parents work together to rear their pups in dens dug in the sand.

MEERKAT

Young meerkats don't know what kind of food to eat, so their mother teaches them. She brings home an insect or a lizard and leaps around in front of the pups until they take the food from her mouth. Sometimes she even brings home scorpions with their tails bitten off so her babies learn how to kill them without getting stung!

FISCHER'S LOVEBIRDS

Lovebirds get their name from the strong bonds formed between males and females, who spend much of their time grooming each other. When it comes time to have a family, the lovebirds build a dome-shaped nest from twigs and bark, where they lay their eggs.

LEOPARD TORTOISE

Baby leopard tortoises use small egg teeth to crack their way out of their shells. Although they hatch from eggs just 1.5 inches (4 cm) across, they can grow to measure more than two feet (0.6 m) long and weigh 80 pounds (36 kg). In captivity, leopard tortoises can live to be 100 years old.

DESERT AND COAST BABIES

Where the Indian and Pacific Oceans meet,

Australia rises above the sea. Most of this land is desert, too dry and scorching hot for most people to live. But even here, baby animals play. Small kangaroos poke their noses out of their mothers' pouches. Baby dingoes wrestle with their brothers and sisters. This wild land also holds miles of sparkling coastline and dense eucalyptus forests. Young koalas learn how to live life in the treetops, and little penguins discover how to march across the beach. Most of Australia's babies are found nowhere else on Earth.

The Duck and the Kangaroo

Said the Duck to the Kangaroo,
"Good gracious! how you hop
Over the fields, and the water too,
As if you never would stop!
My life is a bore in this nasty pond;
And I long to go out in the world beyond:
I wish I could hop like you,"
Said the Duck to the Kangaroo.

II.

"Please give me a ride on your back,"
Said the Duck to the Kangaroo:
"I would sit quite still, and say nothing but 'Quack'
The whole of the long day through;
And we'd go the Dee, and the Jelly Bo Lee,
Over the land, and over the sea:
Please take me a ride! oh, do!"
Said the Duck to the Kangaroo.

III.

Said the Kangaroo to the Duck,
"This requires some little reflection.
Perhaps, on the whole, it might bring me luck;
And there seems but one objection;
Which is, if you'll let me speak so bold,
Your feet are unpleasantly wet and cold,
And would probably give me the roo-
Matiz," said the Kangaroo.

—Edward Lear

The kangaroo is the only large animal that travels by hopping.

KANGAROO | BABY NAME: Joey

GROWS UP: In every habitat in Australia and in the forests of New Guinea

SNACKS ON: Mom's milk, leaves, grasses, flowers, ferns, moss, insects

"I'm famous for my grin. Say cheese!"

On the island of Rottnest, near Perth, Australia, a female quokka is having a snack. Holding a twig in her hands, she nibbles daintily on the leaves. Suddenly, a small head pops out of a pouch in her belly. It's her joey, or baby, and he wants a taste, too!

There are only about 14,000 quokkas in the wild, and most of them live on Rottnest Island. When a Dutch visitor came here in 1696, he thought the creatures he was seeing were large rats, so he named their island "Rattenennest," or "Rat's Nest." But quokkas are actually the smallest member of the kangaroo family: They're about the size of house cats. Like their kangaroo cousins, they carry their babies around in their pouches until their little ones become too big to fit.

Quokkas are social plant eaters that hang out in clans. They seem to like the company of humans, too; trusting and curious, they're known to come up to human visitors to say hello.

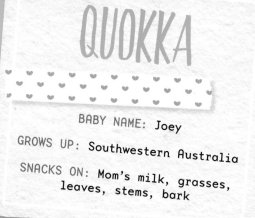

QUOKKA

BABY NAME: Joey

GROWS UP: Southwestern Australia

SNACKS ON: Mom's milk, grasses, leaves, stems, bark

The sugar glider leaps from the top of a tall tree. Holding her arms and legs wide, she stretches the folds of skin that run from wrist to ankle. Suddenly, she's not falling—she's flying! Zooming nearly the length of a football field, the sugar glider finally comes to rest on another tree.

Sugar gliders get their name from their love of sweet tree sap. They glide through the forest from tree to tree, using their large front teeth to chisel through bark to get at the sap inside. As it travels, the sugar glider rubs a special scent on branches. This leaves an invisible trail that its baby can follow through the forest.

Sugar gliders look for food at night, when the darkness protects them from predators. Just before dawn, they head back to the nest. Sugar gliders line their nests with leaves, carrying the foliage there in their coiled-up tails. Groups of up to seven or more adults and babies will share the finished nest, curling up together to keep warm.

SUGAR GLIDER

BABY NAME: Joey

GROWS UP: In forests throughout Australia, Tasmania, Papua New Guinea, and on surrounding islands

SNACKS ON: Mom's milk, nectar, insects, tree sap, pollen, seeds

TO THE RESCUE!

BABY BATS BUNDLE UP

Baby bats love to be held. In the wild, they cling tightly to their mothers, who wrap their wings around their little ones in a protective hug.

But what happens if a baby becomes an orphan? Human rescuers wrap it up in a blanket like a tiny burrito!

Batty for Bats

When a heat wave hit Australia in spring 2014, it left many baby fruit bats without mothers to care for them. Too young to fly, the babies couldn't survive on their own. So rescuers from the Australian Bat Clinic and Wildlife Trauma Centre in eastern Australia stepped in to help.

In the wild, bat mothers give birth to one baby at a time. That's all she can manage: Bat babies weigh about one-fourth as much as their mothers at birth! Even though bats might look like rodents, they're actually mammals that nurse their young,

just like dogs, elephants, and humans. Bats form strong bonds with their mothers, so being away from their protective care and in an unfamiliar place can make bat babies stressed.

At the Centre, rescuers cared for more than 100 little bats around the clock. They gave each baby a rubber pacifier to suck on. They bottle-fed the babies by hand and stroked them gently, mimicking how their mother would groom them in the wild. And they swaddled them in blankets to make them feel comforted and secure.

The Centre takes care of young bats for a few months, until they're ready to be released back into the wild. Then, the young bats will zip through the night, flying freely—as they were born to do.

AN ORPHANED BAT IS WRAPPED IN A BLANKET TO HELP IT FEEL MORE SECURE.

Australia is home to nearly 100 different species of bats.

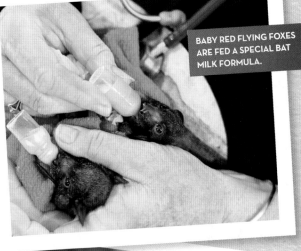

BABY RED FLYING FOXES ARE FED A SPECIAL BAT MILK FORMULA.

BAT BABIES WITH BINKIES

CREEPY OR COOL?

Bats are often seen as creepy creatures of the night. Some people are afraid of bats or think they are bad luck. But they are actually helpful to us! Bats provide natural pest control, eating insects that bother humans. One little brown bat can gobble up 1,000 mosquitoes in a single night!

Despite the saying "blind as a bat," most bats can see. But they do hunt in the darkness of night, never running into a tree or another bat. How do they do it? Bats have a sixth sense called echolocation. As they fly, they make chirping noises too high for humans to hear. The chirps bounce off objects—like rocks, trees, and insects—and echo back to the bat's ears. From these echoes, the bat can figure out the size of the object, how far away it is, where it's moving, and even its texture! Using this amazing ability, bats can navigate through complete darkness.

"After I leave my mom's pouch, I like to ride around on her back."

KOALA

BABY NAME: Joey

GROWS UP: In the eucalyptus forests of southeastern and eastern Australia

SNACKS ON: Mom's milk, eucalyptus leaves

A baby koala was just born. Blind, naked, earless, and about the size of a jelly bean, the baby is completely helpless. Slowly, it climbs through its mother's fur and finds its way to her pouch. It will stay there for about seven months, growing up into a furry, round-eared adult.

They may be as cute as teddy bears, but koalas aren't actually bears. They're marsupials, the family that includes kangaroos, quokkas, and opossums. All marsupials have pouches that keep their young safe.

Koalas live way up high in trees. They have hands and feet specially designed for life in the treetops. Their hands have two thumbs to help them grip tightly onto branches and sharp claws to dig into bark. Their feet have one clawless toe that they use like a thumb, too. Koalas can climb 150 feet (46 m) to the very top of a tree!

During the day, koalas spend most of their time napping—they can sleep up to 20 hours each day! The rest of the time, they spend eating. Koalas eat only one thing: the leaves of eucalyptus trees. Eating the same thing at every meal might sound a little boring. But there are more than 600 different kinds of eucalyptus trees, and to a koala, each one tastes different. To most animals, eucalyptus is poisonous, but koalas have special bacteria in their guts that help them digest the plant.

When baby joeys first start eating eucalyptus, they have a hard time. They go after the leaves with their mouths, only to have their big noses bump them away! It takes a while for joeys to learn to grasp leaves with their hands for snacking.

CASSOWARY

BABY NAME: Chick

GROWS UP: In the tropical forests of northern Australia, New Guinea, and surrounding islands

SNACKS ON: Fruit

In a small hollow in the rain forest floor, five eggs nestle together. They're several times larger than chicken eggs—and bright green! On top of them sits their father: a cassowary, one of the world's biggest birds.

Cassowaries can grow to weigh more than 160 pounds (73 kg). Although they can't fly, they are covered with glossy black feathers that look almost like hair. They have a brightly colored wattle on their neck that can be red, blue, gold, purple, or white.

After the female cassowary lays her eggs, the father takes over the child care. He'll sit on his nest for up to 60 days. When the chicks hatch, they're brown-and-tan-striped fluff balls. But they'll grow up to be formidable fighters: Adult cassowaries have a daggerlike claw on each foot that is up to four inches (10 cm) long. The claw helps them dig through leaves or slice an attacking dingo or crocodile with one swift kick.

Many call the cassowary the most dangerous bird in the world!

The first scientists to see a platypus thought that someone was playing a trick on them. It's one of the world's strangest animals, with the bill and webbed feet of a duck, the tail of a beaver, and the body of an otter. On top of that, males have venomous stingers on the heels of their hind feet!

Platypuses eat by scooping up worms, insects, and shellfish from the bottom of streams and rivers. But they don't have teeth, so they grab some gravel, too, to help them mash up their food. And the platypus has a sixth sense: Its bill can detect electrical signals emitted by living things. That means that they don't need their other senses to hunt.

The platypus even has a strange way of having babies. It is one of only two mammals in the world that lays eggs. (The other egg-laying mammal is the echidna, or spiny anteater.) When she's ready, a female platypus enters a chamber in her burrow in the riverbank, then seals off the entrance. After she lays her eggs, she keeps them warm by holding them against her body with her tail.

PLATYPUS

BABY NAME: Baby platypus

GROWS UP: In the rivers and lakes of eastern Australia

SNACKS ON: Mom's milk, worms, larvae, insects, shellfish

BABY
BUDDIES

ORPHANS BECOME POUCH PALS

When two infant marsupials are missing their mothers, there's only one thing to do: Have them share a pouch!

That's how Anzac the baby kangaroo and Peggy the baby wombat became the closest of cuddle buddies.

Super Snugglers

Anzac the kangaroo was only five months old when he was found in the Macedon Ranges north of Melbourne, Australia, in 2012. Rescuers brought the little kangaroo to the Wild About Wildlife Kilmore Rescue Center in Victoria, Australia. But they thought Anzac seemed lonely. So they introduced him to Peggy, a rescued wombat who was also five months old. Soon, the two marsupials were sleeping together in the same custom pouch made by their rescuers. The babies found comfort in the other's warmth and heartbeat, just as they would have from a mother.

Although they started out about the same size, Anzac and Peggy wouldn't be small enough to share a pouch for long. Adult kangaroos can reach well over 100 pounds (45 kg), and fully grown wombats are half their size, at about 50 pounds (23 kg). And although Anzac would grow up to leap across the landscape at 30 miles an hour (48 km/h), Peggy would rather waddle than run. But as babies, these two orphans showed the world that there's nothing better than a cuddle buddy.

ANZAC AND PEGGY

AWESOME AUSSIES

Both native to Australia, kangaroos and wombats are marsupials, a family of pouched animals. Most marsupials live in Australia, except for one—the opossum, which lives in the Americas. Marsupial babies, called joeys, are born tiny and blind. They crawl to the pouch, where they stay until they have grown enough to come out.

Kangaroos live in herds of 50 or more animals. If they feel threatened, they'll pound on the ground with their big, strong feet. If their foe ignores the warning, the kangaroos will unleash a powerful kick!

Kangaroo babies are just about the size of a grape when they're born. They're not even strong enough to nurse, so the mother kangaroo uses her muscles to pump milk down their throats. At 10 months old, kangaroo joeys are strong enough to leave the pouch for good.

Pudgy, waddling wombats use their claws to dig burrows in Australia's grasslands and eucalyptus forests. Their tunnels can grow to be 640 feet (200 m) long. They come out at night to munch on grasses, roots, and bark. Their teeth never stop growing—a lifetime of chewing on plants keeps them from getting too long. Wombats have pouches like kangaroos, but theirs face backward. That keeps dirt from filling up their furry front pockets when they're digging!

Australia has about 120 species of marsupials.

"My top speed is only about 1.6 miles an hour (2.5 km/h)!"

LITTLE PENGUIN

BABY NAME: Chick

GROWS UP: On the southern coast of Australia and New Zealand

SNACKS ON: Small fish, squid, plankton, krill

When the sun goes down on Australia's Philip Island, the little penguins begin their parade. They march from the shoreline across the beach, heading back to their colony. There, in nests under logs, in rock crevices and caves, their chicks are waiting to be fed.

Little penguins are the smallest penguins in the world. They're also called fairy penguins or blue penguins because of the color of their feathers. They stand just 16 inches (41 cm) tall and weigh only about two pounds (1 kg). Like other penguin species, little penguins can't fly. They use their flippers to soar through the water instead! Little penguins spend the daytime out at sea, hunting for food in the shallow waters close to shore. They wait until the protective cover of darkness to cross the beach and return to their colonies.

Little penguins lay two eggs at a time, and both the parents take turns sitting on the eggs and caring for the babies once they hatch. After two months, the little penguin chicks know how to swim and are ready to enter the sea on their own.

DINGO

BABY NAME: Puppy

GROWS UP: Primarily in Australia, with a few groups in Southeast Asia

SNACKS ON: Milk, meat, rodents, rabbits, birds, lizards, grains, nuts

Once a year, the dingo pack's dominant female gives birth to a litter of puppies. The whole pack works together to raise the little dingoes. Aunties and other female relatives babysit and even nurse the pups. And as the babies grow bigger, all the adults help bring them food to eat.

The dingo's ancestors were domesticated dogs that once lived in Asia. About 4,000 years ago, human travelers brought them to Australia, where they became wild. But dingoes never lost their tie with humans. Today, many dingoes live close to people, eating their food scraps. Sometimes, they hunt sheep and other livestock, making them pests to farmers. To protect their animals, Australian farmers built the world's longest fence—3,488 miles (5,614 km) long—to keep the dingoes away!

Dingoes have one special trait in common with their human companions. Like people, they have wrists that rotate. This allows them to use their paws like hands to catch prey. Dingoes have even been spotted opening doors!

KOOKABURRA | BABY NAME: Chick

GROWS UP: In the eucalyptus forests and woodlands of Australia

SNACKS ON: Mice, snakes, insects, small reptiles, other birds

The loud call of the laughing kookaburra sounds a little like a group of monkeys!

How the Kookaburra Got Its Laugh

ADAPTED FROM AN ABORIGINAL FOLKTALE

The kookaburra was always a very happy bird. Even though he couldn't sing, he didn't feel jealous of those who could.

So when he heard the lyrebird, Australia's copycat, brag that he could sing better than any other bird, the kookaburra wasn't annoyed. But others were. They gathered together and challenged the lyrebird to make good on his boast.

One by one, the challengers sang a tune, warbling as sweetly as they could. But as soon as each one finished, the lyrebird mimicked its song and sang it much more beautifully than his challenger.

The kookaburra watched all this with amusement. He thought it was funny that everyone was trying so hard to sing nicely. The thought tickled the kookaburra so much that at last, he burst out laughing.

The kookaburra's laughter caught the lyrebird's attention. The lyrebird thought the laugh was the kookaburra's song! So the lyrebird tried to imitate it. This made the kookaburra laugh so long and so loudly that the lyrebird could no longer keep up. At last, he was forced to admit he couldn't sing the kookaburra's song.

Even today, the kookaburra can laugh much more heartily than the lyrebird. And when he thinks of this, he laughs so loudly that his happiness rings over all of Australia.

TASMANIAN DEVIL

BABY NAME: Imp

GROWS UP: On the Australian island of Tasmania

SNACKS ON: Mom's milk, birds, snakes, fish, insects, carrion

Snarls fill the night air on the island of Tasmania, off the southern coast of Australia. A Tasmanian devil is on the hunt, and she's come across another devil feasting on a meal that she wants for herself. The two animals face off. They let out spine-chilling screeches. They bare their teeth and lunge at each other. These are Australia's most ferocious animals!

Most people are familiar with the Tasmanian devil from the cartoon character: a growling, ravenous, short-tempered creature. And the real-life animal isn't too different! The world's largest carnivorous marsupial, the Tasmanian devil has sharp teeth and strong jaws that give it, pound for pound, one of the most powerful bites of any mammal.

But the Tasmanian devil's fearsome reputation comes mostly from its feisty personality. Devils will go after just about any animal they cross, including animals much larger than they are, like kangaroos. They'll eat just about anything, too—even roadkill! Devils will swallow every scrap, including hair and bones. And they fight each other ferociously over food.

Tasmanian devils have to be tough from the moment they're born. A mother gives birth to as many as 50 devils in one litter. The tiny, pink babies race each other to the mother's pouch where, inside, there is room for only four of them. The babies, called imps, stay in the pouch for the first 100 days of their lives. Then they ride on their mother's back or stay home in the den while she hunts. After nine months, the young devils are ready to fend for themselves.

Young Tasmanian devils are more agile than older adults. They can climb trees with ease. They like to spend a lot of their time playing, which for a devil means wrestling, biting, and making lots of noise! This rough play helps prepare them to grow up to be Tasmania's top carnivores.

Bandicoot mothers are pregnant with their babies for just about 12 days—the shortest of any mammal! Bandicoots live in almost every area of Australia. Even though they look like large rats, they're actually more closely related to rabbits.

These spotted, cat-size animals have ridges on the bottoms of their feet that help them climb. After young quolls leave the pouch, they use their sharp teeth to hang on to their mother's fur.

BANDICOOT

QUOLL

TOT LOT

More cute creatures from the deserts and coasts of Australia

TREE KANGAROO

GREEN TREE FROG

Very little is known about tree kangaroos, which live only in the rain forest on the island of New Guinea. Scientists think they're solitary animals. Only mothers and their babies form strong bonds, staying together for nearly two years.

Green tree frogs live all over Australia, in forests, wetlands, and even in people's showers and toilet bowls! The frogs lay eggs that hatch into tadpoles. After growing to up to four inches (10 cm) long, the tadpoles transform into frogs.

Brushtail possums are one of Australia's most common marsupials. Some golden brushtails are born with light fur, but these possums are rare in the wild because their fur makes them easy for predators to spot.

GOLDEN BRUSHTAIL POSSUM

BLACK SWAN

Black swans are the state bird and emblem of western Australia, appearing on the state flag. Both the male and female build the nest and raise their babies together.

The bilby is similar to the bandicoot, except for long ears that make it look like a rabbit. Some Australians even want to replace the Easter Bunny with an Easter Bilby!

BILBY

This egg-laying mammal is also called the spiny anteater. It hatches its egg inside its pouch! The baby echidna stays there until its protective spines grow in.

ECHIDNA

FOREST AND STREAM BABIES

In a leafy European forest, baby hedgehogs whistle for their mothers. Under their feet, newborn weasels cuddle together in an underground den. Millions of years ago, great masses of ice moved slowly across this landscape. In their wake, they left miles of waterways: lakes, marshes, fjords, and mighty rivers. The water makes this land rich and green—the perfect home for all kinds of baby animals. From the tops of snow-packed mountains, where baby Alpine ibex move gracefully across cliffs, to the banks of a babbling brook, where little foxes take a drink, the babies of Europe wiggle and waddle across the land.

The Eagle (A fragment)

He clasps the crag with crooked hands;
Close to the sun in lonely lands,
Ringed with the azure world, he stands.

The wrinkled sea beneath him crawls;
He watches from his mountain walls,
And like a thunderbolt he falls.

—Alfred, Lord Tennyson

When diving, steppe eagles can reach speeds of up to 186 miles an hour (299 km/h).

STEPPE EAGLE | BABY NAME: Eaglet

GROWS UP: In steppes, deserts, and grasslands of southeast Europe, southern Russia, Central Asia, and Mongolia

SNACKS ON: Carrion, birds, small mammals

The baby hedgehog trundles across the forest floor. With its spike-covered back, it looks like a pincushion with legs! All of a sudden, the hoglet realizes that it's gotten separated from its mother. Frightened, it lets out a series of high-pitched whistles, and the mother hedgehog comes running. Behind her trail five other pincushions— the hoglet's brothers and sisters.

As they pick their way through the forest, hedgehogs make grunting noises like pigs; that's what gives them their name. Hedgehogs spend their days foraging for worms, centipedes, snails, and other small creatures. Because hedgehogs eat pests, many European gardeners view them as helpful friends. Some even make nests of straw or boxes to entice the prickly critters into their gardens.

Hedgehogs have one of the best defense systems in the animal kingdom: sharp little quills that create a layer of protection around the clever critters. When a threat approaches, they curl up into tiny balls to protect their soft bellies, legs, and faces. Adult hedgehogs can have as many as 8,000 quills!

EUROPEAN HEDGEHOG

BABY NAME: Hoglet

GROWS UP: In woodlands, grasslands, and gardens across Europe

SNACKS ON: Mom's milk, insects, worms, slugs, snails, birds' eggs

A brown hare darts across the grassy field. She leaps in a zigzag pattern meant to befuddle any predators that are watching. She's just come from feeding her babies, and she wants to keep their location a secret.

Baby brown hares, called leverets, are born with their eyes open and full coats of fur. Their mother leaves each leveret in its own shallow depression in the grass, called a form. During the day, the babies stay as still as statues. That makes them hard for hungry predators to spot in the grass. Each night at sunset, the mother comes to feed them.

Once they're grown up, the leverets will be able to run with incredible speed—up to 35 miles an hour (56 km/h). That's fast enough to outrun most predators, like foxes. In the springtime, brown hares show off wild behavior: They chase each other and leap around wildly, and males will even stand up on their hind legs and box each other with their front paws!

BROWN HARE

BABY NAME: Leveret

GROWS UP: In Europe's grasslands

SNACKS ON: Mom's milk, grass, tree bark

TO THE RESCUE!

SCIENTISTS SAVE CUTE KITTIES

In the early 1900s, there were 100,000 Iberian lynx roaming the Iberian Peninsula of southwestern Europe.

But by 2002, there were fewer than 100 of these wild cats left. Experts from the World Wildlife Fund warned that the lynx might die out completely. It would have been the first big cat to vanish from Earth since the saber-toothed tiger went extinct 100,000 years ago. Something had to be done to save the lynx.

Saving the Species

Scientists in Spain and Portugal put their heads together to solve the problem of the disappearing lynx. In 2003, a research center in Doñana National Park of Andalusia, Spain, began breeding captive lynx—something that had never before been done successfully. In 2005, one of the center's female lynx, Saliega, gave birth to three cubs. They were the first Iberian lynx ever born in captivity.

Slowly, more furry lynx cubs were born and soon, centers began setting them free in the wild. Today, the Iberian lynx is now making a comeback. In spring 2016, 48 lynx cubs were born in captivity in centers across Spain and Portugal, and there are now more than 400 Iberian lynx in the wild. Although the lynx's future is still precarious, experts are hopeful that these rare and beautiful cats are here to stay.

Experts believe the Iberian lynx may be the rarest cat in the world.

LYNX CUB FELINA

LIFE AS A LYNX

Many ancient people thought of the lynx as a mythical creature. In Greek and Norse myths, lynx can see what others can't and reveal hidden truths.

Wild lynx don't have mythical powers, but they do have keen vision and hear very well with their distinctive black-tipped, tufted ears. Weighing up to 27 pounds (12 kg), lynx make their homes in forests and sand dunes. When the winter snows blow in, lynx rely on their large fur-covered feet, which act like snowshoes and allow the cats to run lightly on top of the snow without sinking in. Lynx give birth to two or three kittens at a time, and the mother takes care of them until they're nearly two years old.

LYNX CUBS BREZO AND BRISA

WEASEL

BABY NAME: Kit

GROWS UP: Across Britain, throughout much of Europe, and in parts of Asia and North America

SNACKS ON: Mom's milk, small mammals, birds

The weasel takes off across the grass. She's spotted one of her favorite meals: a mouse. Her prey cornered, the weasel stops the chase and begins to roll, spin, jump, and twist. The mouse watches, fascinated. It's distracted, and it doesn't realize the dancing weasel is inching closer until—chomp!—it's too late.

The weasel picks up her prey and carries it back to the den, where she has hungry babies to feed. Weasels are always hungry. To survive, they have to eat about half their body weight every day! That has made these creatures fierce hunters. They're Britain's smallest native carnivore, just about eight inches (20 cm) from nose to tail. With their long, slender shape, weasels can follow prey animals into their burrows. They mostly eat small mammals like voles and rats, but they've been spotted taking on rabbits 10 times their size.

When there is a lot of prey around, weasels will often kill more than they can eat. They dig holes near their dens and keep them stocked with the extra food. That makes it easy for weasels to grab a snack whenever they get hungry. And during the winter, when prey is scarce, these food stores act like natural refrigerators, keeping food fresh so that weasels can survive days without finding a new meal.

Along with their relatives, stoats and ferrets, weasels are famous for the strange and silly dance they sometimes perform while hunting. Scientists think the dance probably helps confuse the target, making it easier for the weasels to get close to their prey. But weasels have also been spotted dancing when there's no prey around. So maybe, like people, weasels dance for a different reason—because it's fun!

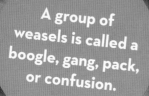

A group of weasels is called a boogle, gang, pack, or confusion.

ALPINE IBEX

BABY NAME: Kid

GROWS UP: In the European Alps

SNACKS ON: Mom's milk, plants, grasses

"Hanging out way up here keeps me safe from predators."

High up in the mountains of northern Italy, the Cinigo Dam rises 160 feet (49 m) above the rocky landscape below. This rock wall is nearly vertical. People on the road above point at some shapes that dot its face. The shapes are moving—they're Alpine ibex, and somehow they are clinging to the impossibly steep surface!

To human onlookers, the ibex's climb looks like a death-defying feat. But it's just an everyday activity for these animals, a type of wild mountain goat that lives in the mountains of the European Alps. Ibex are some of the best climbers in the world. Their bodies are engineered for the job, with split hooves with a sharp rim that grips on rock outcrops and a soft center that sticks on smooth surfaces.

Ibex are grazing animals, but they also need minerals, such as salts, that they can't get from plants. Experts think that's probably why the ibex living near the Cinigo Dam venture up the steep wall, to lick up salts that collect there. Mothers and their babies—ibex often have twins!—can often be seen perched on the rocky wall, casually licking up a salty snack, with the ground far below.

The baby badger hops back and forth in front of its mother. The badger family has just come out of the den, and it's time to play! The other cubs—four altogether—join in, and soon all the babies are frolicking in the light of the setting sun.

Badgers are nocturnal animals, meaning they are most active in the evening. They hunt in the darkness, looking for earthworms—their favorite food. One badger can eat several hundred earthworms in a single night! They use their strong legs and sharp claws to dig a maze of tunnels and chambers up to 109 yards (100 m) long. These burrows, called setts, are their homes, and badgers spend the daytime snoozing there.

Badgers will line their setts with grass and leaves to make cozy beds, and they keep them clean by maintaining a separate chamber to use as a bathroom. Often, more than one badger family, or cete, will live together in a sett. Badgers inherit setts from their parents and are always busy renovating their homes, refining them and adding new tunnels. Some badger setts have existed for centuries!

EURASIAN BADGER

BABY NAME: Cub

GROWS UP: In woods throughout Europe to eastern Russia, China, and Japan

SNACKS ON: Mom's milk, earthworms, larvae, slugs, snails, bird eggs, fruit, small mammals

SHEEPDOG BECOMES BABYSITTER

Three times a day, Jess heads out to take care of the orphaned lambs on her farm.

She gets a bottle full of milk and sets out for the fields. She goes even if it's pouring rain outside; after all, the babies have to eat. This wouldn't be unusual behavior for a farmer. But Jess is a dog!

Lending a Paw

Jess, a springer spaniel, has been helping out around the farm her whole life. Her owner, Louise Moorhouse, who owns the farm in Devon, England, taught Jess how to hold the milk bottle in her mouth when she was just a puppy.

Moorhouse raises 270 sheep on her 180-acre (73-ha) farm. Normally, female sheep—called ewes—take care of nursing their babies. But once in a while, a mother won't be able to care for her baby. To survive, the lamb must be fed milk from a bottle. On most farms, a human farmer takes on that task, but on Moorhouse's farm, Jess has decided that it's her job. When she's not busy bottle-feeding little lambs, Jess helps out Moorhouse with other farming duties. She carries buckets of feed to the adult sheep and delivers equipment to her owner.

Jess's hard work doesn't go unnoticed. The sheep show their appreciation by nuzzling their canine caregiver, giving the devoted dog a well-deserved tummy rub. And the sweet spaniel loves the attention!

JESS FEEDS AN ORPHANED LAMB.

Each dog has a unique nose print—just like a human fingerprint.

"THAT TICKLES!"

HUMAN'S BEST FRIEND

If your own pet dog will barely sit on command, Jess the farm dog may seem a bit odd. But dogs have been helping out humans for thousands of years.

Dogs are descended from the gray wolf, and scientists believe they made the switch from fierce predators to snuggle buddies about 32,000 years ago. The transformation likely began when wolves started hanging around humans to snack on their scraps. Soon, they were begging for food, and before long, they were domesticated dogs that helped protect their humans, hunt for their meals, and herd their livestock.

111

The baby red deer hides in a clump of tall grasses. She was born just a few days ago, and she won't be ready to join the herd until she's two weeks old. Her coat is dotted with white spots. This coloring helps her blend in to the forest floor, where sunlight filters through the leaves, creating a dappled pattern. Over the next few months, her spots will start to fade as she gets her adult coat.

Red deer are the largest native land mammals in the United Kingdom. Stags, or adult male deer, can stand 4.5 feet (1.4 m) high at the shoulder and weigh more than 400 pounds (182 kg). Red deer like to live in the forest, where they can spend their days eating all kind of plants, from grasses to trees.

Red deer usually spend their time alone. But in October, the breeding season begins. Stags compete for females by roaring and crashing their antlers together. Their antlers are made of bone and can grow as much as an inch (2.5 cm) in a day! Each winter, the stags lose their antlers and begin growing them again to be ready for the fall.

RED DEER

BABY NAME: Calf

GROWS UP: In woodlands, forests, and grasslands in the United Kingdom

SNACKS ON: Mom's milk, grasses, heather, shrubs, trees

DORMOUSE

BABY NAME: Pup

GROWS UP: In the woodlands of southern England and Wales

SNACKS ON: Mom's milk, buds, nuts, berries, insects

The baby dormouse climbs up a tree, gripping the bark with his front paws, his rump wiggling as he moves his way up the trunk. He's practicing skills he'll need when he grows up. Dormice are known to be agile climbers, but it's rare to spot one in action: They're shy animals that like to stay hidden.

Even though they have round ears and long tails, dormice aren't really mice; they belong to the same family as squirrels and beavers. Dormice spend much of their time up high in trees, eating buds, nuts, berries, and insects. They can go their entire lives without ever touching the ground! In the winter, dormice begin to hibernate—or go into a deep sleep. They're one of the animal kingdom's longest sleepers, spending up to three-quarters of their lives snoozing!

In the summer, dormice build nests of bark that they strip from honeysuckle bushes. A female dormouse can give birth to up to seven young, and dormouse families are very close-knit, playing, wrestling, and snuggling just like human relatives.

"I pollinate flowers by carrying pollen on my whiskers."

Red foxes are members of the dog family and are known for their intelligence and cunning.

FOX | BABY NAME: Kit, pup, or cub

GROWS UP: In forests, grasslands, mountains, and deserts across the Northern Hemisphere

SNACKS ON: Mom's milk, fruits, berries, grass, birds, small mammals, insects

The Fox and the Crow

**ADAPTED FROM A MEDIEVAL
ENGLISH FOLKTALE**

On a fine summer's day, Fox was out for a stroll when he spotted Crow sitting high up in a tree. He noticed that Crow had a very large chunk of cheese in her beak. Fox hadn't had his breakfast yet, and the sight of Crow's cheese made him very hungry. So he sat down at the foot of the tree, trying to think of a way he could trick Crow and get the cheese.

Crow looked nervously down at Fox, for she had heard tales of his cleverness. But she knew foxes didn't climb trees, so she felt safe up on her high perch.

"My, my," said Fox to Crow. "What a magnificent bird you are! Your feathers are simply glowing in the sunlight, and your beauty is beyond compare!"

"However," Fox went on. "I have heard from my friends that your voice is your finest feature of all. I have been longing to hear you sing, and how lucky for me that I've walked beneath your tree today!"

Crow was very flattered by Fox's compliments. She had never given much thought to her voice, but surely this fine gentleman must be right! Forgetting her suspicions, she opened her mouth and started singing a tune. "Caw! Caw! Caw!" she said. And as she did so, of course, down fell the cheese right into Fox's waiting mouth.

Quick as a flash, Fox swallowed the cheese. Grinning up at Crow, he said, "Well mistress, you do indeed have a lovely voice. If only your brain was quite as fine!"

Female brown bears give birth to their babies during the hibernation months, when they're safe from predators. The babies are born blind and naked, weighing just 12 ounces (340 g). From this tiny size, they grow up big and strong: Males can reach 800 pounds (363 kg)!

EURASIAN BROWN BEAR

This wildcat, descended from the domestic house cat, is often mistaken for a large tabby. Fluffy, mewing wildcat kittens grow up to be fierce hunters that aren't afraid to go after animals much larger than they are, from other cats to small deer.

EUROPEAN WILDCAT

TOT LOT

More sweet little ones from the forests and streams of Europe

CHAMOIS

These goatlike animals are mountain dwellers that can run 31 miles an hour (50 km/h) and jump 20 feet (6 m). Females and their babies live together in herds. While they graze, another chamois stands guard. If she senses danger, she stomps her feet and calls with a high-pitched whistle to put the herd on guard.

When a great gray owl wants to win over a female, he brings her a dead vole held in his beak. When the female lays her eggs, she stays with the eggs at all times while he brings food to her—and later, to their chicks.

GREAT GRAY OWL

This colorful bird looks like it belongs in a tropical rain forest, but it makes its home in central and southern Europe. These birds live up to their names, eating mostly honeybees. It's one of the few birds that have help feeding their young: Often, sons or brothers of the parents will help out with catching bees and bringing them to the chicks.

EUROPEAN BEE-EATER

EUROPEAN PINE MARTEN

These shy and elusive members of the weasel family like wooded areas where they can nest in hollow trees and the abandoned homes of other animals. Their babies are born in March or April and begin to emerge from their dens by June to start learning how to live on their own.

RED SQUIRREL

Red squirrels raise their young—called kittens—in globe-shaped nests made of twigs and lined with moss and grass. They build their nests high up in trees to keep their kittens safe from predators like foxes that lurk below. Red squirrels often build more than one nest a year, and if one becomes infested with fleas, they simply move out!

EUROPEAN BISON

The magnificent European bison—the largest land animal in Europe—was wiped out in the wild in 1919. But calves were carefully raised from animals kept in zoos around the world, and in 2016, the first adult bison were reintroduced to their old land. Conservationists hope they'll spread across the country once again.

TROPICS AND PEAKS BABIES

In Asia, woolly baby yaks

play high in the mountain ranges. A small snow leopard treads softly through a blowing blizzard. This land is home to some of the planet's tallest peaks and largest plateaus. Here, too, are island nations, where the constant drip of rain creates some of the lushest tropical forests on Earth. The tangle of leafy branches is the perfect playground for young orangutans to swing and for tiny tarsiers to peer through the leaves with their wide eyes. From camouflaged chameleon hatchlings to boldly black-and-white panda cubs, meet some of the babies that squeak, whistle, and roar across the planet's largest continent.

The Rhinoceros

SO this is the Rhi-no-ce-ros!
I won-der why he looks so cross.
Per-haps he is an-noyed a bit
Be-cause his cloth-ing does not fit.
(They say he got it read-y made!)
It is not that, I am a-fraid.
He looks so cross be-cause I drew
Him with one horn in-stead of two.

Well, since he cares so much for style,
Let's give him two and see him smile.

—Oliver Herford

Three species of rhinoceros live in Asia, and two more live in Africa.

RHINOCEROS | BABY NAME: Calf

GROWS UP: In grasslands and forests of India

SNACKS ON: Mom's milk, grasses, branches, leaves, fruits, aquatic plants

SLOW LORIS

BABY NAME: Infant

GROWS UP: In the tropical rain forests of Southeast Asia

SNACKS ON: Mom's milk, insects, eggs, small mammals, plants

Blinking its big, round eyes, the slow loris moves through the jungle. She grabs onto tree branches with her strong fingers and toes, climbing in search of insects to snack on. Her twin babies are parked on a branch of a nearby tree, waiting for their mother to return from hunting.

Slow lorises are shy animals that hide during the day. When one is spotted, it freezes and raises its arms above its head, covering its face. This may look adorable, but experts think the slow loris puts on this peculiar pose for a reason: It's one of the few venomous mammals in the world. The slow loris has two glands inside its front elbows that release a toxin. When the animal feels threatened, it raises its arms and licks the glands, mixing the toxin with their saliva. That gives the critter a nasty bite.

Experts think this toxin may have a second purpose: to keep babies safe. When slow lorises lick their young, they might be spreading the toxin to their little ones' fur, giving them a poisonous coating that protects them from predators. If one of the babies does find itself in distress, it lets out high-pitched chirps that make its parents come running.

The red panda cubs roll around their den, chewing on bamboo twigs their mother brought them. Snowy white rings are growing in on their wide, fluffy tails, and their paws are sprouting with fur that will help them climb wet, slippery branches in the bamboo forest.

Although red pandas live alongside giant pandas in China's bamboo forests, they aren't closely related to the black-and-white bears. Red pandas are about the size of a small dog, with a kitten-like face and fur the color of cinnamon. They are acrobats that use their claws for gripping and their bushy tail for balance as they move through the trees. Red pandas love to climb way up to the top of the forest canopy for a sunbath.

A few days before a female red panda has babies, she builds a den in a hollow tree, stump, or rock crevice. She lines it with leaves, grass, and moss to make it soft and comfortable. Her cubs are born with their eyes tightly closed, and mom keeps them safe in the den until they're about three months old. Then they begin to explore their mountain home.

RED PANDA

BABY NAME: Cub

GROWS UP: In the bamboo forests of south-central Asia to southern China

SNACKS ON: Mom's milk, bamboo leaves

TO THE RESCUE!

PLAYTIME FOR PANDA CUBS

At the Chengdu Panda Base in Chengdu, China, teetering toddler pandas clown around on a slide.

They follow their human caregiver up the stairs and then, one by one, roll and tumble down the incline. Some go headfirst; others crash into each other, making a fluffy black-and-white-panda pile at the bottom. But these cuddly creatures aren't just adorable, they're also important: They represent new hope for saving their species.

Panda Party
The Chengdu Panda Base is one of the most famous places in the world to catch a glimpse of these cuddly creatures. It covers 600 acres (243 ha) in the heart of the pandas' natural habitat. Thousands of visitors flock there every year to see the pandas sleeping, eating, and playing.

In autumn and winter, newborns fill the nursery at the Chengdu Panda Base. They're tiny and helpless, weighing 900 times less than adults. At first,

rescue workers bottle-feed the babies, but soon the cubs are strong enough to grasp the bottles in their chubby paws and feed themselves. Before long, they're ready to head outside to spend their days romping, wrestling, and even playing on the slide! Researchers watch closely as the young bears grow. What they learn will help them figure out how to help save the wild cousins of their little charges from extinction.

Once the panda cubs have grown up, the Chengdu Panda Base sends them to zoos around the world, where they help raise awareness about China's beloved bears and their fight for survival. When they have raised enough pandas in captivity, the Chengdu Panda Base plans to begin releasing them back into the wild. Hopefully someday, these playful panda cubs will spend their days munching on bamboo in China's wild forests.

"WHEEEEE!"

Pandas feast on bamboo. They eat up to 40 pounds (18 kg) of the leafy greens each day!

PANDAS LOVE TO PLAY.

PROTECTING PANDAS

Centers like the Chengdu Panda Base give tourists a place to see Asia's iconic animal face to face. But they also have an important mission: helping save a species that is struggling to survive. Giant pandas live high up in only a few of central China's cool, misty mountain ranges. As humans move into their forests, there is less and less room for pandas to live. And female pandas give birth to a cub only once every two years, so populations grow slowly. In 2003, there were only 1,600 of the animals in the wild.

But recently, pandas have gotten some good news. Conservationists have created protected areas in China's bamboo forests where wild pandas can live and breed. And now, their numbers are starting to grow: A 2014 study counted 1,850 wild pandas, and experts estimate that by 2016, that number rose to 2,060. The panda's fight for survival isn't won yet, but this progress shows that helpful humans can change the fate of struggling species. That's great news for the panda and for all of Earth's endangered animals.

"In the Malay language, my name means 'person of the forest.'"

ORANGUTAN

BABY NAME: Infant

GROWS UP: In the rain forests of Southeast Asia

SNACKS ON: Mom's milk, fruit, leaves, flowers, bark, honey, insects

High up in a tree, a young orangutan is trying to build a nest. She grabs a branch and weaves it through another, but her handiwork falls to the ground. Orangutans build a new nest to sleep in every night. But nest building is a tricky skill that takes a long time to learn: Young orangutans begin practicing when they're six months old, and they don't master it until they're age three or four.

These reddish orange primates are close relatives of humans, and like their human cousins, they're very intelligent. Orangutans have mental maps that tell them when each tree in their forest home produces fruit to eat. They've been seen using large leaves as umbrellas to stay dry during rainstorms. And they use body language and their voices to communicate: A squeaky kissing sound shows excitement; a deep "grumph" warns of danger.

Whereas all other apes and monkeys on Earth are social animals that live in groups, orangutans spend a lot of their time alone. But mothers and their infants form one of the strongest bonds of the animal kingdom. Young orangutans nurse for as long as seven years! Males may stay close to mom for a few years after that, and young female orangutans often stick near mom into their teens. They learn parenting skills by watching their mothers care for their younger siblings.

Orangutan babies are born with pink faces and tufts of orange hair that stick straight up. They spend their first few weeks clinging to their mother's belly as she swings through the forest. As they grow bigger, they switch to riding piggyback so they can see what's going on. They watch their mother closely, studying how to find fruit, build nests, and all the other abilities they'll need to live a long life in the forest. There's a lot to learn!

High in the mountains of Nagano, Japan, snow surrounds a pool of water made steamy by heat deep underground. Like human bathers enjoying a hot tub, a troop of Japanese macaques sits in the water. While mothers relax, their babies splash each other.

Japanese macaques are native to Japan, where they live farther north than any other primate on Earth, except for humans. Their thick fur allows them to put up with temperatures as low as minus 4°F (-15.6°C). But when the temperature really drops, these monkeys head to the hot springs.

Many monkey species have complicated social systems, with some members of the troop out-ranking others. For Japanese macaques, the females are in charge. Female macaques inherit their rank from their mothers. And like humans, they can also pass along culture from one generation to the next. In the 1980s, scientists saw one young monkey washing her sweet potato in seawater before eating it—maybe to give it a nice salty seasoning. This monkey taught her new trick to her family, and, although she died years ago, her troop still washes its food today.

JAPANESE MACAQUE

BABY NAME: Infant

GROWS UP: In the forests of Japan

SNACKS ON: Mom's milk, fruit, insects, ferns, roots, bird eggs

INDIAN PARADISE FLYCATCHER

BABY NAME: Chick

GROWS UP: In forests across Asia

SNACKS ON: Insects

A male Indian paradise flycatcher swoops through the forest. With his long tail streaming behind him, he snags a fly out of midair. It's the perfect snack to bring back to his four chicks waiting in the nest.

Indian paradise flycatchers are only about eight inches (20 cm) long. But they're easy to spot despite their small size because of their colorful plumage. Females have a blue head and neck with rust orange wings and tail. Males can look similar, but most have long streamer feathers on their tail and bright blue rings around their eyes. Sometimes males are black and white instead.

Mother and father Indian paradise flycatchers share the duties of parenthood. They work together to build nests made of twigs bound together with spiderwebs. They take turns sitting on the eggs, and when the eggs hatch, both parents help feed and protect the baby flycatchers.

A LION, A TIGER, AND A BEAR—OH MY!

Because tigers live in Asia, lions in Africa, and black bears in North America, the three species don't usually cross paths.

Though sad circumstances brought this unlikely trio together, they formed a friendship so strong it lasted the rest of their lives.

Rescue Mission

Police officers in Atlanta, Georgia, U.S.A., were investigating the basement of a local house in 2001 when they came upon a shocking sight: three cubs, all less than a year old. Meant to grow up in the forests and jungles of their natural habitats, they were trapped in small cages, malnourished and suffering from injuries.

The three little critters were taken to Noah's Ark Animal Sanctuary in Locust Grove, Georgia, an organization that cares for more than a thousand animals every year. Caretakers named them Baloo the bear, Leo the lion, and Shere Khan the Bengal tiger, and set about nursing them back to health.

The first step was a surgery to repair a wound on Baloo. The procedure went perfectly, but when Baloo was taken away from the group for treatment, the other two animals became distressed. They had grown to depend on each other during their ordeal. The keepers realized that in order to make sure these animals were happy, they could never separate them. The trio was tied for life.

Predator Pact

All three animals made complete recoveries. Normally dominant creatures that would have fought each other on sight, the friends developed a strong bond. They shared toys, romped and rolled together, and ate together. They even groomed each other, licking each other's fur and rubbing noses. And when it was time for a snooze, they loved to snuggle. Even though the three animals lived in a large, three-acre (1.2-ha) enclosure, they were never far apart. The story of the animals that turned an awful situation into a lifelong friendship inspired everyone who visited them.

A hungry tiger can eat as much as 60 pounds (277 kg) in one night.

THE TRIO LOVED TO SNUGGLE ...

... AND TO PLAY TOGETHER.

WILD THINGS

Bengal tigers are big, black-and-orange-striped cats that live in small pockets in India. Bengal tigers' coloring helps them blend into the tall grasses or forest vegetation where they live. With inch-long (2.5-cm) claws and three-inch (7.6-cm)-long canine teeth, Bengal tigers are mighty hunters. But as newborn cubs, they're small and helpless. Their mother leaves her litter of up to seven babies alone when she heads into the forest to find food for them. At just two months old, the cubs begin joining her on the hunt.

TARSIER

The mother tarsier clings to the tree branch with her long fingers, holding her baby gently in her mouth. Her huge eyes scan the forest, looking for a tasty insect. Like an owl, she turns her head backward as she searches the trees.

Tarsiers have a stare like no other animal on Earth. They have the largest eyes relative to body size of any mammal: Each eyeball is bigger than the tarsier's brain! Their eyes are so big that they can't rotate them. Instead, they turn their neck 180 degrees to look around. Tarsiers silently wait and watch for prey to come close. Then they make their move. These tiny hunters can leap 40 times their body length, grabbing bats and birds right out of the air.

At birth, tarsier babies' weight is about a third of their parents'. They are born fully furred and with their eyes wide open. They're able to climb when they're just one day old—ready to spend a life in the trees!

"I'm a wild yak. Humans use domestic yaks to pull heavy farm equipment and carry large loads."

YAK

BABY NAME: Calf

GROWS UP: In the mountains of Central Asia

SNACKS ON: Mom's milk, grasses, herbs, wild flowers

The young yak nibbles on grasses in a field. She's surrounded by plants and flowers: It's summer, the season of plenty on the world's highest and largest plateau. She's learning how to graze, but she stays close to her mother in case she wants a drink of milk.

Yaks are huge animals—males can weigh nearly 2,000 pounds (907 kg). Yaks have horns and dark brown, shaggy fur—and a herd of wild yaks is an impressive sight. When winter comes, they'll need their thick coats for protection: It can get below minus 40°F (-40°C) in these mountains. Hail and snowstorms beat down on the land here. This extreme place is sometimes called "the roof of the world."

In the winter, food is scarce. Yaks will travel great distances to find enough to eat. They use their thick horns to break through the snow and ice to get to the plants underneath. By then, yak calves have grown strong. Surviving in this extreme place means that they've got to be tough!

SNOW LEOPARD | BABY NAME: Kitten

GROWS UP: In the mountains of Central and South Asia

SNACKS ON: Mom's milk, ibex, goats, sheep, hares, birds, carrion

Unlike many other big cats, snow leopards can't roar.

The Legend of the Snow Leopard

**ADAPTED FROM
AN ANCIENT FOLKTALE**

In the 11th century, the poet and saint Milarepa traveled to small caves and through remote villages. He would stop during his trek to meditate, but he craved solitude. He needed to go far, far away to escape his worldly distractions. So he decided to set off for a magical cave deep in the mountains.

At that time, winter was coming and, with it, the howling winds and pounding snows. Milarepa's disciples, or followers, feared for his safety. They begged him to stay. "Surely you can wait until spring to make your journey," they told him.

But Milarepa was determined. And he went anyway. Shortly after he walked into the mountains, it began to snow. It snowed for 18 days and 18 nights. A thick, white blanket piled up on the mountain trail, and it didn't clear for six months.

Milarepa's disciples feared for their great leader's life. But with hope in their hearts, they went to search for him when the mountains cleared in spring. After many days of hiking, the disciples were almost to the cave when they sat down to take a rest. In the distance they saw a snow leopard sitting on a big rock. They followed the leopard's tracks down the trail. But there, they saw something strange: Where the snow leopard's tracks ended, human footprints began.

As they approached the magical cave, they heard someone singing. It was Milarepa! When he saw them, he smiled and said, "What took you so long? You reached this part of the mountain a while ago."

"How did you know we were here?" asked the disciples.

"I saw you when I was sitting on the rock," said Milarepa.

"We saw a snow leopard sitting there," said the disciples. "But we did not see you."

"Ahh," said Milarepa. "I was the snow leopard."

And so, the disciples learned that Milarepa was not just a man but also a mystical spirit who could change himself into the snow leopard. This is how the great Milarepa survived the winter, meditating in the cave as a man and transforming into the great feline hunter to search for food in the winter storm.

Your average house cat might hate water, but not so for fishing cats! Despite their stocky bodies, they swim like pros with the help of webbing between their toes. Fishing cats learn to fish from their mothers, scooping prey out of the water with their paws.

FISHING CAT

CHAMELEON

Chameleons are best known for their ability to change their color. But they also have eyes that move independently, so that the lizard can look at two things at once. Chameleon babies begin to hunt a few days after they're born. They use their long, sticky tongue to snag insects.

TOT LOT

More bouncing babies from the peaks and tropics of Asia

BINTURONG

Binturongs have a face like a cat's, a body like a bear's, and a tail like a monkey's. These odd animals spend most of their time climbing trees, using their tail like an extra hand. Baby binturongs are born with their eyes tightly closed, and they hide in their mother's shaggy fur for the first few days of life.

KOMODO DRAGON

They may not really be dragons, but Komodo dragons are the world's largest living lizards. An ancient species, the Komodo dragon has ancestors that date back more than 100 million years. Komodo dragon eggs are the size of grapefruits.

BACTRIAN CAMEL

Camels are legendary for their ability to travel long distances across the desert without food or water. By surviving on fat stored in its hump, a camel can go a week without drinking and several months without eating. Baby camels don't have humps—just patches of curly hair that show where humps will grow.

COBRA

The female cobra lays a clutch of eggs and then stays close by, guarding them from predators. With her loud hiss, she warns hungry enemies not to get too close to her venomous fangs. Baby cobras are able to strike as soon as they hatch.

SLOTH BEAR

Despite what their name suggests, sloth bears can actually run pretty fast—even faster than a human! Like tree sloths, they do like to hang upside down on tree branches. Sloth bears have long, thick hair that comes in handy when they have cubs, which grab on tight to hitch a ride on mom's back.

DHOLE

The dhole (pronounced "dole") looks like a fox, but it's actually a wild dog. Female dholes can have as many as 12 pups in a litter. Dholes are cooperative animals—they hunt together, and all the dholes in the pack help take care of the pups.

ICE AND SNOW BABIES

In the polar regions,

snow and ice stretch in a blanket of white as far as the eye can see. Fierce storms make winds scream and temperatures drop far below zero. Yet even here, baby animals bounce, wiggle, and thrive. Down south in Antarctica, fuzzy, gray emperor penguin chicks nestle on top of their fathers' feet to stay off the chilly ice. Up north in the Arctic Circle, polar bear cubs follow their mothers across the landscape, sliding and spinning on their rumps. Bundle up to meet some of the tots of snow and ice—the babies of the polar regions.

Seal Lullaby

Oh! hush thee, my baby, the night is behind us
And black are the waters that sparkled so green.
The moon, O'er the combers, looks downward to find us
At rest in the hollows that rustle between.
Where billow meets billow, there soft by the pillow.
Oh, weary wee flipperling, curl at thy ease!
The storm shall not wake thee, no shark shall overtake thee
Asleep in the storm of slow-swinging seas.

—Rudyard Kipling

Harp seals are born on floating sea ice.

Arctic foxes have the biggest litters of any wild animal in the world.

ARCTIC FOX

BABY NAME: Pup

GROWS UP: In the tundra of Alaska, Canada, Greenland, Iceland, northern Europe, and Russia

SNACKS ON: Mom's milk, lemmings, voles, squirrels, small birds, eggs, berries, fish

The arctic fox sits motionless on the snow while the wind whistles across the tundra. It's cold out here, but the fox has a built-in scarf: His fluffy tail is curled around his face to protect him from the frigid wind. He's watching for signs of prey moving through the snow. Once he catches something, he'll bring it back to the den, where his pups and their mother wait.

Arctic foxes are known for their pure white coat. But their fur actually changes color with the seasons. In the winter, it's white to help the fox blend in with the snow. When the snow melts away in spring, the fox sheds its winter coat, showing gray fur that helps camouflage the animal against the rocks and dirt.

Each spring, female arctic foxes give birth to a litter of pups. They can have as many as 14 at a time! The male fetches food for his family and guards the den over the summer. Then, it's time for the pups to head out onto the tundra on their own.

A young reindeer noses through the snow, looking for tasty shoots to eat. He's two years old, and his antlers are just beginning to sprout on top of his head. They look like little hairy buds, but in a few years, they'll grow into a mighty rack. In most deer species, only the male grows antlers. But some female reindeer grow antlers, too!

Reindeer are perfectly suited for life in their subzero home. Their noses warm the air they breathe. Their fur traps air, helping keep their bodies warm. Even their feet are made for the cold: In the summer, when melted snow makes the ground wet, their foot pads soften, giving the reindeer extra grip. In the winter, the pads tighten, so the reindeer can use the sharp rims of their hooves to get a foothold on the slippery ice.

Reindeer milk is rich in nutrients to help young calves grow quickly. Calves double their weight by the time they're two weeks old! By six months, they're eating mosses and plants. In the winter, when greens grow scarce, reindeer survive by nibbling on the lichen that grows on rocks under the snow.

REINDEER

BABY NAME: Calf

GROWS UP: In the tundra and forests of Canada, Alaska, Greenland, northern Europe, and northern Asia

SNACKS ON: Mom's milk, mosses, herb, ferns, grasses, leaves, lichen

143

TO THE RESCUE!

SCIENTISTS GET A BIRD'S-EYE VIEW

The penguin chick makes its way across the Antarctic ice toward a colony of emperor penguins.

As the chick nears, the black-and-white birds turn to watch it. One even waddles up to it for a closer look.

To the penguins, the newcomer looks like any other fluffy, gray penguin baby. But it's not—it's actually a robot with a hidden camera inside!

Chick Cam

Warming temperatures are melting the sea ice in Antarctica, the only place in the world where emperor penguins live. To learn how to help the penguins survive, scientists are studying their habits. But penguins are shy creatures, and they get scared when scientists get too close.

One researcher, Yvon Le Maho from the University of Strasbourg in France, thought there had to be a better way. Could he find a way to get an up-close look inside a penguin colony without stressing the birds?

In 2013, Le Maho teamed up with filmmakers to design a "chick cam." It had the fluffy feathers and gray coloring of a baby emperor, but inside, it held a secret camera. The team members sent it wheeling toward an emperor colony—and held their breaths. But the penguins didn't blink! They treated the robotic penguin like a real chick.

After a year on the ice, the chick cam collected more than 1,000 hours of footage. Now, Le Maho and his team are working on a design for an adult-size version of the chick cam, which will carry more equipment and film the colony at any time of year, not just when there are chicks around. Le Maho and his team plan to use the footage they gather to better understand the travel and mating patterns of these majestic emperors of the ice—and hopefully, help them stay in the Antarctic for good.

An adult emperor penguin is about the same height as a six-year-old human.

PARENTING ON ICE

Emperor penguins make their home in one of the harshest places on Earth. Wind chills on the Antarctic ice can reach minus 76°F (-60°C). To survive here, penguins use teamwork: They huddle together to stay warm. Each penguin takes a turn in the toasty inside of the huddle. Once a penguin on the inside has warmed up, it gives up a spot to a chilly friend and moves to the outside of the group.

Female penguins lay their eggs in the wintertime. Then, the hungry mothers take off on a hunting trip. Some have to travel 50 miles (80 km) to reach the sea and the fish, squid, and krill they eat. When moms leave, the father penguins take over. They balance their eggs on their feet to keep them off the ice and cover them with a flap of feathered skin. For two months, the father penguins babysit, eating nothing and waiting out the storms.

Finally, the mothers return, with bellies full of food that they regurgitate for their newly hatched chicks. Their daddy duty done, the fathers head for the sea to get a meal of their own.

EMPERORS GROW TO BE THE LARGEST OF ALL PENGUIN SPECIES.

POLAR BEAR

BABY NAME: Cub

GROWS UP: On the sea ice of Canada, Russia, Alaska, Greenland, and Norway

SNACKS ON: Mom's milk, seals

"I can smell seals from a mile (1.6 km) away."

It's October in the Arctic, and a pregnant polar bear is digging her den. Using her huge paws, she scoops out a snowbank. She'll need the shelter: When she has her cubs in the winter, temperatures outside may drop to minus 58°F (-50°C). Inside her cozy den, it will stay as much as 40 degrees warmer.

The cubs will grow into some of the largest land carnivores on Earth. Male adult polar bears can measure more than 10 feet (3 m) tall! But at birth, they're helpless. They're pink and hairless, their eyes are closed, and they weigh just a pound (.45 kg). Their mother keeps them warm and feeds them rich milk that helps them grow quickly. By April, the cubs are ready to leave the den.

To survive in the Arctic, they'll have to become skilled hunters. Polar bears rely on seals as their main source of food. But on the flat sea ice, it's hard to sneak up on prey. So polar bears will sit motionless outside a seal's breathing hole—sometimes for hours—waiting for their prey to surface.

Polar bears may be fierce, but they have a playful side, too. They've been spotted sliding down icy slopes just for the fun of it! Sometimes, two bears will spend several days together, playing and traveling. But most of the time, polar bears live alone on the ice.

Most bears hibernate in the winter: They hole up in dens underground and enter a sleeplike state. Their breathing and heart rate slows, and their body temperature drops. But polar bears don't hibernate when winter comes: They keep hunting seals no matter the weather. Mother polar bears do enter dens when it's time to have their babies. To prepare, they eat as much as they can to pack on weight. Then, they live off their fat stores until their cubs are old enough to venture outside. To keep their babies warm and fed, polar bear mothers go without food or water for as long as eight months.

SNOWY OWL

BABY NAME: Chick

GROWS UP: On the Arctic tundra

SNACKS ON: Lemmings, small mammals, birds

The male snowy owl floats across the tundra, making no sound. In his beak, he carries a small, furry lemming. He lands next to a female owl, raises his wings, and leans forward. He's trying to woo her. If all goes well, she'll soon find a small hollow in the tundra to lay her eggs in.

Snowy owls are one of the Arctic's most majestic creatures. With a wingspan nearly five feet (1.5 m) wide, they soar across the landscape, their striking white feathers blending in with the snow below them. Using their sharp eyesight and hearing, they can find prey that's hidden under plants—or even under the snow. Their favorite food is lemmings: A snowy owl can eat more than 1,600 of these rodents a year!

Snowy owls often won't have babies when food is scarce. Instead, they wait until a time when there is plenty to feed their chicks. While the mother stays with the babies, the father hunts. He provides for his family until the chicks are about 10 weeks old and ready to take flight across their cold, snowy home.

"I may look like a bear, but I'm actually the largest member of the weasel family."

The wolverine snarls as she runs across the winter landscape. Her enormous paws are like snowshoes, with claws that dig into the ice. She's spotted a potential meal—the carcass of a moose. The dinner belongs to a 500-pound (227-kg) black bear—but the 30-pound (14-kg) wolverine doesn't care. The fearless creature is going to steal the meal! She grabs part of the carcass and runs off with it before the bear can stop her.

As she settles in to eat, her cubs appear. They have to watch their mother to learn how to find food. Adult wolverines will attack animals many times their size, such as caribou. They'll fight creatures much bigger than they are, like bears and wolves, for a meal. And they have hearty appetites, devouring every part of their prey—right down to the bones.

Wolverines roam vast distances in search of food: In 2009, researchers tracked one that traveled an astonishing 550 miles (885 km) in two months, crossing highways, mountain ranges, and state lines. Because they're always on the move, wolverines are difficult to study. Much remains a mystery about these fierce predators of the north.

WOLVERINE

BABY NAME: Kit

GROWS UP: In the tundra and forests stretching up to the Arctic

SNACKS ON: Mom's milk, deer, sheep, rodents, hares, scavenged carcasses

BABY BUDDIES

SEAL AND PENGUIN SHARE A LAUGH

What did the penguin say to the elephant seal?
"Hey, what happened to your trunk?"

Penguins and seals don't normally cross paths in Antarctica. That's why a traveler had to stop and snap a picture when he spotted a gentoo penguin chick and an elephant seal pup that looked like they were sharing a joke.

Frosty Friends

Gentoos may not normally buddy up with elephant seals, but they do like company. They live in groups called colonies on the rocky coast. One gentoo colony can have thousands of penguins! And gentoo penguins form close attachments with their partners, often mating for life. Male gentoos have romance down to an art: Once a male finds a female he likes, he will search the area for the smoothest pebble he can find to present to her.

If the female accepts him as her mate, she will take the love token and place it on her nest.

Elephant seals, on the other hand, usually like to spend their time alone—that is, until breeding season arrives in the fall. Then, male seals will gather groups of up to 50 females. Female elephant seals are about six times smaller than the massive males. While they're nursing their pups, elephant seal mothers don't eat. Instead, they live off the energy stores in their blubber.

When winter comes, elephant seals return to the chilly Antarctic waters to feast on squid and fish. Although their cousins, the leopard seals, do eat penguins, elephant seals are not penguin predators. That could be why the young gentoo felt safe enough to come up to his seal friend on the beach!

LIFE AT THE SOUTH POLE

Gentoo penguins are known for their bright orange beak, their adorable waddle, and the white band across the top of their head. They're the third largest penguins in the world, standing at 30 inches (76 cm). Gentoo parents work together to build a circular nest made of stones, grass, moss, and feathers. They take turns sitting on the eggs and then caring for the chicks when they hatch.

Southern elephant seals are the largest seals on Earth. Full-grown males can be more than 20 feet (6 m) long and weigh up to 8,800 pounds (4,000 kg). Elephant seals may not have a trunk exactly like an elephant's, but the male elephant seal does have a long nose. When he wants to intimidate other males, he inflates his nose with air and makes a loud bellowing sound to show how big and strong he is.

"THAT'S A GOOD ONE!"

Despite its frozen landscape, Antarctica is actually a desert.

"Aaaaooooo! My howl is how I talk to my pack mates."

ARCTIC WOLF

BABY NAME: Pup

GROWS UP: In northern Canada and Alaska, parts of Greenland, Iceland, and northern Europe

SNACKS ON: Mom's milk, seals, foxes, arctic hares, birds, salmon, rodents

An arctic wolf pokes her nose out of her den in the snow. Behind her, 12 pups whimper for her. But she has to eat. Making no noise, the pure white wolf pads out across the moonlit snow to find a meal.

In the Arctic Circle, where these wolves live, the sun does not rise for five months out of the year. But the darkness is no problem for this elite hunter. Working together, a pack of arctic wolves can bring down a caribou or musk ox. Such a large animal is enough to feed the whole pack for several days. The pack will help the mother wolf take food back to her pups in the den.

Arctic wolf puppies are born with white fur, and they stay white into adulthood. The color helps camouflage them in their snowy home. Unlike most other wolves, which have yellow eyes, arctic wolves' eyes are dark brown to help protect them from the bright glare of sunlight off the snow.

It's spring, and the puffin's beak is beginning to turn from gray to a vivid striped orange—earning it the nickname "sea parrot." These arctic birds likely use their bright beaks to help them attract mates.

Each year during mating season, Atlantic puffins land on rocky cliff tops on the coast to build their nests. Puffin couples often choose the same site year after year. When a chick hatches, its parents head to the water to hunt for small fish. Puffins are swift swimmers. They use their wings to "fly" underwater and can dive down 200 feet (61 m)! Once they've caught a meal, they carefully carry it back to their babies in their large beak.

Puffins are fast in the air, too. They flap their wings up to 400 times per minute and can reach speeds of 55 miles an hour (89 km/h). They spend most of the year at sea, flying to their nest sites when it's time to lay eggs. Scientists aren't sure how these bright birds find their way: They could use landmarks, smells, or maybe even the stars to guide them.

PUFFIN

BABY NAME: Puffling

GROWS UP: In Atlantic seas and coasts

SNACKS ON: Small fish

WALRUS | BABY NAME: Calf

GROWS UP: Near the Arctic Circle

SNACKS ON: Mom's milk, shrimp, crabs, tube worms, soft corals, sea cucumbers, mollusks

Adult male walruses can weigh as much as a car.

How the Walrus Came to Be

ADAPTED FROM A FOLKTALE OF THE CHUKCHI PEOPLE OF SIBERIA

In Chukchi legends, the Raven is a sacred bird. Inside him lives the spirit of the creator god, who made the first people of the wind and grass. But this god is also a mischievous trickster, and many tales tell of his craft and cunning.

One day, the Raven decided that the world had been in darkness too long. He wanted the sun to light it up. There was just one problem: The sun belonged to someone else. But the Raven was smart, and he was determined to get the sun for himself.

So the Raven took to the sky. He flapped his wings and flew far, far away to a distant country. There he came upon a house. Inside, there was a man who watched over the sun, moon, and stars. The man had sewed them up inside sealskins, making them into balls for his little daughter to play with.

When the Raven arrived, the little girl was outside in the front yard. The Raven said to her, "Little girl, bring your sun-ball outside so we can play with it." Excited to have a playmate, she ran inside and begged her father for the ball. "You can't play with the sun-ball today," he said. "But here is the ball of stars."

The little girl ran outside with the ball of stars and, excited to play, tossed it to Raven. He grabbed it, but then, instead of tossing it back, he threw it up with all his might high into the air. The ball burst open, and the stars flew out and stuck to the sky.

"Oh no," said the Raven. "Look what I did! Clumsy me. You'd better go inside and get another ball." The little girl ran inside and came back with the ball containing the moon. But Raven promptly repeated his trick! So the girl went back inside once again, and this time, when her father wasn't looking, she grabbed the last ball, the one with the sun inside. Once again, the Raven threw the ball toward they sky. The sun burst out of its sealskin and stuck there, lighting up the world for the first time.

When the man found out that his moon, stars, and sun were gone, he was very upset. Sorry that she had disobeyed her father, the little girl ran far away, down to the ocean, crying as she went. As she dove into the water, she was transformed into a walrus. And where the tears ran down her face and dripped down her nose, she sprouted long walrus tusks. That's how the sun got into the sky and how the walrus came to be, too.

Baby arctic hares grow quickly: They're born in springtime, and by the fall, they're nearly adults. They have to be big and strong by the time the cold winter hits. Arctic hares have lots of traits that help them hold in body heat, like their thick fur and short ears. Their fur turns white in the wintertime.

ARCTIC HARE

MUSK OX

Musk oxen have lived in the Arctic for thousands of years, and they have their survival strategy down pat. When predators threaten them, the herd will form a circle around their babies, with their sharp horns facing outward.

TOT LOT
More wiggling, waddling little ones from the ice and snow of the poles

CANADA GOOSE

Baby Canada geese have been known to follow almost anything that moves—including dogs and humans!—thinking it to be their mother. Their parents lead them to the water to learn to swim before they're 24 hours old.

ALBATROSS

Once young albatrosses learn to fly, they leave the land behind until they're about five years old. When they're ready to have chicks of their own, they return to the land. These giant birds ride the ocean winds with their enormous wings—which span up to 11 feet (3.5 m)!

Baby ermine are born covered with fine white hairs that grow into beautiful fur coats. By eight weeks of age, they're able to hunt with their mother. Ermine are aggressive predators that use their long, slim bodies to slip through animal burrows underground.

ERMINE

MOOSE

A moose calf can outrun a human by the time it's just five days old. It will grow into a huge animal that can be 6.5 feet (2 m) tall at the shoulder and weigh 1,800 pounds (820 kg). Despite their giant size, moose are swift runners and good swimmers that can stay underwater for 30 seconds at a time.

LEMMING

Baby lemmings are born in burrows under the snow that shelter them from the cold Arctic winters. Once they grow up, they'll spend about six hours a day searching for buried bulbs, shoots, and roots.

DALL SHEEP

Young male Dall sheep look like the females until they reach the age of three. Then, their horns begin to grow. The horns grow in the spring, summer, and fall and stop growing during the winter. This creates a pattern of rings on the horns—one for each year of the Dall sheep's life.

OCEAN AND SEA BABIES

Dive beneath the water

that covers more than two-thirds of Earth's surface and you'll discover an underwater world teeming with babies of the sea. There are more kinds of baby animals here than anywhere else on Earth! In coral reefs near the coast, clownfish fathers watch their tiny eggs hatch. Dolphin pods swim and frolic and, out at sea, 10-foot (3-m)-long baby humpback whales swim at their mother's sides. And in the deepest, darkest parts of the sea, strange creatures like the piglet squid wiggle their tentacles. These are the babies that float, paddle, and swim in the world's oceans.

We Fish

We fish, we fish, we merrily swim,
We care not for friend nor for foe.
   Our fins are stout,
   Our tails are out,
As through the seas we go.

Fish, Fish, we are fish with red gills;
Naught disturbs us, our blood is at zero:
We are buoyant because of our bags,
Being many, each fish is a hero.
We care not what is it, this life
That we follow, this phantom unknown;
To swim, it's exceedingly pleasant,—
So swim away, making a foam.
This strange looking thing by our side,
Not for safety, around it we flee:—
Its shadow's so shady, that's all,—
We only swim under its lee.
And as for the eels there above,
And as for the fowls of the air,
We care not for them nor their ways,
As we cheerily glide afar!

We fish, we fish, we merrily swim,
We care not for friend nor for foe:
   Our fins are stout,
   Our tails are out,
As through the seas we go.

—Herman Melville

"We like to live in large schools above coral reefs."

SEA GOLDIE | BABY NAME: Fry

GROWS UP: In the Indian and Pacific Oceans

SNACKS ON: Zooplankton

"When space gets tight in the reef, I get a roommate! I don't mind sharing my anemone home with another clownfish."

CLOWNFISH

BABY NAME: Fry

GROWS UP: In tropical coral reefs

SNACKS ON: Algae, plankton, mollusks, small crustaceans

A clownfish father hovers near his nest of eggs in a coral reef. He fans them to make sure they get enough oxygen-rich water. He checks them for signs of fungus and eats any damaged eggs to prevent disease from spreading to the others. He fusses over his eggs for a whole week.

Then, the eggs hatch. The baby clownfish are transparent and very difficult to see. They float away and spend about 10 days adrift. After that, they settle to the bottom of the sea to hunt for an anemone to call home.

Anemones look like plants, but they are actually animals in the same family as jellyfish. They attach to underwater rocks or shells and wave their stinging tentacles in the ocean current. They wait for tiny plankton and fish to swim by and then grab them.

Clownfish have a special talent: They're immune to the poison in the anemone's tentacles. They make their home right inside the stinging anemone! The clownfish and its anemone form a strong bond; the clownfish brings food to the anemone and cleans parasites off of it. In return, the anemone provides a home for its fishy friend.

First thing in the morning, a male and female seahorse meet in the floating kelp forest. Seahorses mate for life, and they greet each other every day with a courtship dance. They swim and spin together for several minutes before separating for the rest of the day.

This daily dance isn't the most unusual trait seahorses have. When a seahorse pair has babies, it's the father that carries the eggs and gives birth! Like a kangaroo, he has a pouch on his front. He keeps the eggs safely inside until they hatch, releasing miniature seahorses into the water.

Although the seahorse babies are each no bigger than a grain of rice, they're totally on their own from the moment they're born. They feast on newly hatched brine shrimp to grow bigger and stronger every day.

Even when they're fully grown, seahorses are some of the world's slowest swimmers. The only way they can move forward is by fluttering a small fin on their back. So when seahorses want to go far, they hitchhike! With their monkey-like tails, they grab on to floating seaweed to travel long distances.

SEAHORSE

BABY NAME: Fry

GROWS UP: In shallow tropical and temperate waters around the world

SNACKS ON: Plankton, small crustaceans

A dolphin mother has just given birth to a brand-new baby calf. Using her snout, mom carefully nudges her little one toward the surface so he can take his very first breath.

Dolphins live in the water, but they're not fish; they're mammals that breathe air and nurse their young. Calves stay close by their mothers, swimming in mom's slipstream. That helps them save energy that they need for growing: During their first six months of life, dolphin calves can gain as much as three-quarters of a pound (0.3 kg) every day!

Bottlenose dolphins are highly social animals that love one another's company. They travel together in groups of 10 to 40 dolphins called pods. They communicate with each other using squeaks and whistles. They talk with body language, too—snapping their jaws, slapping their tails on the surface of the water, and sometimes leaping as high as 20 feet (6 m) in the air!

Dolphins are extremely intelligent animals. Some experts believe they are Earth's second smartest creature, after humans. Dolphin brains are very similar to our own, with a large area devoted to complex thoughts like problem-solving and self-awareness. Dolphins use their smarts to help them hunt: They've been seen blowing "bubble nets" around schools of fish to herd them into a group for easy eating. When they've had enough to eat, dolphins love to spend their time socializing and playing. One of their favorite games is playing catch with a piece of seaweed.

Each member of a dolphin pod has its own unique whistle. These whistles are like names—dolphins use them to identify each other. Pregnant dolphins even sing their own "names" to their unborn calves. Experts aren't totally sure why they do it, but they think it may help mother and baby bond.

Dolphins are born with hair only on top of their rostrum (beak). It falls out soon after birth.

BOTTLENOSE DOLPHIN

BABY NAME: Calf

GROWS UP: In tropical and temperate oceans worldwide

SNACKS ON: Mom's milk, fish, squid, crustaceans

TO THE RESCUE!

SEA TURTLES WEAR SWIMSUITS FOR SCIENCE

In 2015, a team of scientists released a group of sea turtles into the ocean.

Anyone paddling nearby when the shelled swimmers entered the water caught a strange sight: These turtles were wearing swimsuits!

Scat Secrets

The turtles' snappy swimwear was a creative solution to a problem that had left the researchers scratching their heads: how to collect turtle poop. Scientists gather animal poop, or scat, all the time—it's one of the best ways to find out what an animal's been eating, where it's been traveling, and whether it's healthy.

A group of researchers at Australia's University of Queensland wanted to figure out where local logger-head turtles were looking for food. These sea turtles are endangered, and the scientists knew that protecting areas where the turtles feed could help protect the turtles, too.

Scientific Solution

To figure out where the loggerheads were feeding, the scientists needed to collect the turtles' scat. So they gathered six loggerhead turtles, put them in a tank, and waited for them to go. But the turtle poop dissolved as soon as it hit the water, making it impossible to gather. The scientists needed a better way to save the scat.

One of the researchers had an idea. He went to a secondhand store and bought rash guards—the swim shirts surfers wear to protect them from scrapes and sunburns. Then, the scientists got to work with needle and thread, fashioning the material into custom turtle swimwear. Once slipped over the shell, the swimsuits worked perfectly at holding a turtle "diaper" in place.

The scientists suited up the turtles and waited to collect their samples. Afterward, they removed the suits and set the turtles free in Moreton Bay, off the coast of Australia. The scientists repeated the procedure with new groups of turtles for a year, and then began to study their results. They'll use what they learn to determine which sea turtle feeding areas need more protection.

READY FOR A SWIM?

TURTLE TROUBLES

One of the largest turtle species in the world, loggerheads can reach three feet (1 m) long and weigh about 250 pounds (113 kg). Every two to four years, loggerhead females head to the beach to nest—the only time in their lives they leave the ocean. A female loggerhead turtle will drag herself up the beach, dig a pit with her back legs, and lay between 50 and 200 eggs the size of golf balls. She will then cover up the nest and leave her babies to hatch.

Loggerheads swim in every ocean in the world, but their survival is threatened. As people have moved to the beaches where they lay their nests and fished in the places where sea turtles hunt for food, the turtles' numbers have dropped. Protecting these areas is one way to help make sure turtles continue to swim in the seas far into the future.

Sea turtles return to the beach where they were born to lay their eggs.

BACK TO THE SEA!

PUFFERFISH

BABY NAME: Fry

GROWS UP: Across the world's oceans

SNACKS ON: Algae, clams, mussels, shellfish

The pufferfish is swimming along peacefully when suddenly, a hungry shark appears in front of her. Oh, no! The shark lunges, snapping its jaws, and—poof! The pufferfish swallows a huge gulp of water and instantly inflates into a ball three times her normal size. Outwitted, the shark swims away.

Even if the shark had managed to snag the pufferfish before it inflated, it wouldn't be a smart snack. Pufferfish contain a deadly poison in their skin and organs. A single pufferfish is toxic enough to kill 30 humans! Even so, the fish is considered a delicacy in Japan, where specially trained chefs prepare it for customers looking for a dinnertime thrill.

When a female pufferfish is ready to give birth, she heads to the water's surface to release her eggs. The eggs are so light that they float on the water until they hatch, about a week later. And although the mother pufferfish doesn't stick around to protect her babies, she does leave them with a gift: a coating of her poison. If a predator gulps up one of the petite puffers, it spits the baby right back out!

"I'm also known as a blowfish. Can you guess why?"

An octopus mother guards her eggs: thousands of small, white dots clinging to a rock on the ocean floor. She covers her babies with her body and defends them from predators. She sends gentle currents rolling over them to make sure they get enough oxygen. Hatching the eggs is a labor of love; it may take months or even years of dedicated work. And the mother octopus never leaves them, even to eat.

Her eggs hatch all at once, the sea filling with tiny baby octopuses. They're only a few millimeters at first, but they'll grow fast—some species of octopus can be more than four feet (1.2 m) long.

Octopuses have a large brain and know how to use it. They're able to find their way through mazes, solve problems, and take things apart for fun. They've even been seen using tools—carrying coconut shells to hide inside when shelter is scarce.

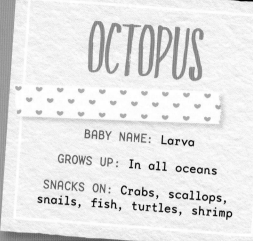

OCTOPUS

BABY NAME: Larva

GROWS UP: In all oceans

SNACKS ON: Crabs, scallops, snails, fish, turtles, shrimp

SWEET SEA LION SEEKS SIDEKICK

The custodian at a restaurant in La Jolla, California, U.S.A., got a big surprise when he vacuumed the dining room early in the morning on February 4, 2016.

A baby sea lion was sitting quietly at one of the booths!

Restaurant workers at the Marine Room, an oceanfront eatery, weren't sure how the little sea lion had snuck in. But the cute pup looked just like it was waiting there for its dining companions. Head chef Bernard Buillas sent out photos of the sea lion sitting politely at the booth and staring out the window at the ocean waves, joking that the baby sea lion "was a little bit early for his high tide breakfast reservation."

Surprise From the Sea
California sea lions are some of the most social animals on Earth. They love to hang out in groups called colonies. Hundreds might come together to loll around on a sandy beach, bathing in the sun. But they don't often go looking for companionship at restaurants!

Employees at the Marine Room called officials at nearby Sea World for help. The team identified the baby sea lion as a female, about eight months old. At 20 pounds (9 kg), she was very small for her age. Maybe she had come to the restaurant looking for a nice meal!

Sea World officials named the pup Marina, after the restaurant. They took her in, fed her, and watched over her. Eight weeks later, the little pup had more than doubled her weight. She was fit and healthy. Her team of caretakers released her back into the wild. Now Marina swims and frolics with other sea lions in her ocean home. Maybe the next time she drops by the Marine Room in search of a snack, she'll bring a sea lion friend with her!

Sea lions
can gallop.

CHECKING OUT THE WAVES

SEA LION SECRETS

Sea lions may look slow and clumsy on land, but that's because they're made for the water. With their sleek shape and strong flippers, they can reach speeds of 25 miles an hour (40 km/h). Sea lions have special nostrils that close up when they dive, allowing these aquatic animals to stay under for nearly 10 minutes at a time. This skill comes in handy when they're chasing the fish, squid, and shellfish that make up their diet.

When they're not deep-diving, California sea lions like to spend their days on the beach. In La Jolla, California, where Marina the pup was discovered, tourists love to watch the local sea lions basking on the beach.

ORCA

♡♡♡♡♡♡♡♡♡♡♡♡♡♡♡♡♡♡

BABY NAME: Calf

GROWS UP: In oceans around
the world

SNACKS ON: Mom's milk, seals,
sea birds, squid, octopuses,
sea turtles, sharks, fish

A group of adult orcas surrounds a newborn underwater. Working together, they use their snouts to push the baby toward the surface where it can catch its first breaths. Orcas are very attached to their offspring. Mothers have been known to surface around a research boat with their newborns in tow, as if to show off their babies.

Orcas are the largest members of the dolphin family. Males can grow to nearly 33 feet (10 m) long. Sometimes called killer whales, they're one of the world's most powerful predators, dining on large animals like sea lions and sharks. They've been seen snatching seals right off the ice!

Orcas live in groups called pods, which can have as many as 40 members. These intelligent animals work together to hunt, just like wolf packs. They also communicate with clicks, whistles, and pulses. Each orca family has its own call, which it passes down to its offspring. When a new calf is born, the orcas repeat the call to the baby, and the calf listens and learns to sing its family song.

Within a few minutes after it's born, the baby manatee is already swimming. Although adult manatees travel in single file, babies stick close by their mothers' sides.

Manatees are sometimes called sea cows for their bulky bodies and slow way of moving. And, just like land cows, manatees are vegetarians that spend all day grazing. One manatee can eat a tenth of its body weight in a single day. That's a lot of sea grass and weeds: Manatees can weigh as much as 1,300 pounds (600 kg)!

In the past, manatees' gentle nature and lazy pace made them easy targets for hunters. Today, manatees are protected by law, but they still face dangers from motorboats and fishing nets.

Manatees live in shallow rivers, in bays, and along coasts. They don't like to get too chilly, preferring waters that are above 68°F (20°C). During winter, they head to the Florida coast to spend the season in balmy waters. In summer, they migrate as far north as Cape Cod, Massachusetts. Despite their large size, manatees are graceful swimmers that use their powerful tails to travel. They have even been known to body surf when playing!

MANATEE

BABY NAME: Calf

GROWS UP: Along the North American East Coast, the Amazon River, and rivers of Africa

SNACKS ON: Mom's milk, sea grasses, weeds, algae

"I'm a relative of the elephant. Do you see the family resemblance?"

Whale songs can travel underwater for thousands of miles.

WHALE | BABY NAME: Calf

GROWS UP: In temperate waters of the Atlantic and Pacific Oceans

SNACKS ON: Mom's milk, zooplankton

Why Whales Don't Live in Lakes

Many years ago, whales swam in the world's lakes, but today, they live only in the oceans. And for that, you might blame Paul Bunyan, the giant lumberjack of American folklore.

Once, Paul and his fellow lumberjacks were up in Michigan. They had hundreds of logs to move downriver to Lake Erie. But it had rained so long and so hard there that the whole river had turned to mud. The lumberjacks sat around their campfire and complained. "There's no way we'll be able to float these logs down through this river of mud," they said.

Paul knew he had to think of something. He took his big blue ox, Babe, and went out for a walk on the banks of Lake Huron. There, Babe began to play with the whales. Using her massive horns, Babe uprooted pine trees and tossed them into the water. The whales leaped above the surface, caught those trees in their mouths, and tossed them right back. That made Paul wonder. "Could the whales be tamed?" he thought.

So Paul went back to camp and began to make preparations. He took great sheets of leather. And while the rain poured and poured down, Paul stayed up all night, cutting and sewing that leather into enormous bridles and saddles.

The next morning, Paul called to Babe and said, "Bring those whales close to shore." Babe tossed a few pine trees in close, and the whales swam toward the shore. Paul waited there, ready to earn the trust of the mighty beasts. In his hand he held a special food he'd made called snooze, all gooey and fishy, just what whales love to eat. Paul held out the snooze to the nearest whale and said, "Come on, attaboy. Come here and try this delicious snooze."

Shyly, the whales came closer and closer. They lifted their snouts above the water and sniffed that salty, fishy snooze. It made their mouths water, and they swam closer still. Soon, all the whales were nibbling on the snooze. And when Paul slipped those bridles over their heads and those saddles on their backs, they didn't seem to mind. Paul grabbed the whales' reins and began to lead them upriver toward the camp. The water was mostly mud, but a whale is a strong, mighty creature. And so on they swam.

When Paul and his herd of whales came up to camp, the lumberjacks there couldn't believe what was before their eyes. "One man to a whale, men," said Paul. The lumberjacks each grasped the reins, and swung astride the giant beasts. Then, Paul threw a log into each whale's snapping jaws. "Not even mud can stop us from a log drive!" he cried. "Let's go!" The lumberjacks rode the huge whales through the river of mud, each great beast with a log clenched tightly in its giant mouth. When they reached the lake, the men unloaded all those logs, and Paul set those whales free.

It was a great day, except for just one thing. That herd of whales decided they didn't much like being saddled and made to work. So they swam up and away. They jumped the Niagara Falls and swam toward the saltwater. And those whales never did come back to the lakes again.

SEA OTTER

BABY NAME: Pup

GROWS UP: Along the coasts of the Pacific Ocean in North America and Asia

SNACKS ON: Mom's milk, mussels, clams, sea urchins, crabs, squid, octopuses, fish

"Our fur is coated in a special oil that makes us waterproof!"

The mother otter dives deep under the waves and grabs a clam and a small rock from the ocean floor. She swims to the surface and floats on her back. Using her belly like a table, she bashes the rock against the clam until it pops open and then gobbles up the tasty treat inside. Sea otters are one of the few animals on Earth that use tools.

When baby sea otters are first born, they can't swim on their own. They have an extra-buoyant coat that keeps them from drowning, but the helpless pups can easily float away on the current. So when it's time for the mother to hunt, she wraps her baby in seaweed to anchor it in place.

When she's not hunting, the mother otter takes her baby with her everywhere, holding it on her chest. The pup watches its mother closely, copying her every move. This way, the baby otter quickly learns to swim and hunt for itself—survival skills that it will need to live a long life in the ocean.

Unlike other ocean-dwelling mammals, sea otters don't have a thick layer of blubber, or fat, to keep them warm. So they wear the world's thickest fur coat. Every square inch of a sea otter's body is covered with more than a million hairs. In comparison, you've probably got fewer than 100,000 hairs on your whole head!

Sea otters spend most of their time floating on their back in the ocean, grooming, eating, and playing. They like to hang out together, with females and their pups in one group and male sea otters in another. When it's time to nap, sea otters often wrap themselves in seaweed to keep from drifting away while they snooze—or sometimes they hold hands while sleeping!

177

This spiky fish has a nasty surprise waiting for any critter that tries to snap it up: poison in the spines on its body. But their eggs don't have this defense system. So after lionfish parents release their eggs into the water, they quickly hide before any lurking predators catch on.

More than 4,500 kinds of crabs live in all the world's oceans. When crab eggs hatch by the thousands, they drift away on ocean currents. As the tiny crab grows, its hard shell gets too tight, and the crab sheds it and grows another one.

LIONFISH

CRAB

TOT LOT
More small swimmers that paddle and dive in the world's oceans and seas

NARWHAL

JELLYFISH

Narwhals are nicknamed "unicorns of the sea" for the swordlike tusk on the male's head. This "tusk" is actually a tooth that grows right through the narwhal's upper lip! Narwhals spend about half the year in the cold water under the Arctic ice. In summer, they move to coasts to give birth.

Even though jellyfish have no heart, no brain, and no blood, they've lived on Earth for 650 million years—way before there were dinosaurs! There are many kinds of jellyfish, some bigger than a human and others as small as the head of a pin. Jellyfish babies begin as larvae that settle to the bottom of the ocean, then sprout into what looks like a plant. The "plant" buds, releasing young jellyfish into the ocean.

SEA STAR

Most sea stars have five arms, but there are species in the ocean with 10, 20, and even 40 arms! Sea stars usually reproduce by laying eggs, but they have another nifty trick, too: If a part of their body is cut off, they can grow the piece into a whole new sea star.

STINGRAY

Even though stingrays have eyes, scientists don't think they use them for hunting. Instead, they have a sixth sense: They track their prey by detecting the tiny electrical signals they emit. When baby stingrays are born, they look like tiny adults, and they're able to fend for themselves from birth.

MORAY EEL

Moray eels may look like snakes, but they're really fish. These shy animals spend most of their time hiding in holes in rocks and coral on the ocean floor. Moray eels can lay 10,000 eggs at a time, which float near the surface of the ocean. It can take them a year to grow big enough to swim down to the ocean floor.

PIGLET SQUID

The ocean's strangest creatures lurk far below the surface, in the depths where there's darkness and intense pressure. Many of the animals that live there are barely understood, like the piglet squid. Measuring just 3.9 inches (10 cm) long, this petite and roly-poly creature has a special organ that produces light so that it can see at the bottom of the sea.

Till To-Morrow.

Good night! good night!—the golden day
  Has veiled its sunset beam,
And twilight's star its beauteous ray
  Has mirrored in the stream;—
Low voices come from vale and height,
  And murmur soft, good night! good night!

Good night!—the bee with folded wings
  Sleeps sweet in honeyed flowers,
And far away the night-bird sings
  In dreamy forest bowers,
And slowly fades the western light
  In deepening shade,—good night! good night!

Good night! good night!—in whispers low
  The ling'ring zephyr sighs,
And softly, in its dreamy flow,
  The murm'ring brook replies;
And, where yon casement still is bright,
  A softer voice has breathed good-night!

Good night!—as steals the cooling dew
  Where the young violet lies,
E'en so may slumber steal anew
  To weary human eyes,
And softly steep the aching sight
  In dewy rest—good night! good night!

—J. C. Yule (Pamela S. Vining)

WHERE DO YOUR FAVORITE BABY ANIMALS LIVE?

You've read about critters that swing from trees in the rain forest, graze in the grasslands, and scamper across the ice. Those animals are adapted to live in certain climates and conditions; they inhabit a "biome"—a community of plants and animals that share a particular habitat. This map shows the location of different biomes across the world.

NORTH AMERICA

Atlantic Ocean

Pacific Ocean

SOUTH AMERICA

BIOMES

- Desert
- Forest
- Grassland and savanna
- Ice
- Tropical rain forest
- Tundra

Arctic Ocean

EUROPE

ASIA

AFRICA

Pacific
Ocean

Indian
Ocean

AUSTRALIA

ANTARCTICA

MORE ON FOLKTALES

MOUNTAINS AND PLAINS BABIES

"Why the Porcupine Has Quills" is adapted from a folktale of the Ojibwe people.

The Ojibwe are one of the largest Native American Indian tribes in the United States. They're known for the strong, light canoes they built of bark from the birch tree. They're also famous for their storytelling: They have passed down folktales like this one from generation to generation.

RIVER AND RAIN FOREST BABIES

"The Legend of the Pink Dolphin" is adapted from a folktale from the Amazon region of Brazil.

Legends are an important part of the local culture there. Some explain the origins of local fruits like acai. Others are tales about the mysterious creatures that live in the area, like the giant anacondas that coil up in the river's shallows and the pink dolphins that swim through its waves.

JUNGLE AND SAVANNA BABIES

"How the Zebra Got Its Stripes" comes from a legend told by the San people.

The San people have lived in southern Africa for 20,000 years, making them the oldest inhabitants of the area. They are the ancestors of the ancient humans who first came to be in Africa. Like many cultures, the San don't write down their history, but they pass along stories like this one through storytelling.

DESERT AND COAST BABIES

"How the Kookaburra Got Its Laugh" is based on a folktale from the Aboriginal, Australia's indigenous people.

They have lived in the area for 45,000 years or longer, making them one of the oldest cultures in the world. The ancient Aboriginal lived across the continent of Australia, surviving by hunting the animals and gathering plants to eat. They have a rich culture of dances, rituals, and myths like this one.

FOREST AND STREAM BABIES

"The Fox and the Crow" is adapted from a folktale from medieval England.

Tales still popular today, like the story of Robin Hood and the legend of King Arthur, also come from this era. Some folktales were fantasies that told of ghosts and fairies. Others—like this one—were meant to teach a lesson. Modern historians study folktales to learn about the culture and beliefs of ancient people.

TROPICS AND PEAKS BABIES

"The Legend of the Snow Leopard" comes from the mountains of Asia.

Many cultures in this part of the world revere the snow leopard as a mystical creature. They believe that the animal is a mountain spirit who can shape-shift at will. That's probably because of the cats' shy and secretive natures: Although they live in 12 countries, snow leopards are almost never seen. And if someone is lucky enough to see one, it's just a glimpse—before the wild mountain cat seems to disappear into the snow.

ICE AND SNOW BABIES

"How the Walrus Came to Be" is adapted from a folktale of the Chukchi people.

The Chukchi are an Arctic people who live in the extreme northeastern part of Siberia, Russia. Those who live in the interior make their living by herding reindeer. Those who live on the coast hunt sea mammals like seals, sea lions, and walruses. Their most famous myths are about the creation of the Earth and its animals.

OCEAN AND SEA BABIES

"Why Whales Don't Swim in Lakes" is based on a folktale of the American West.

It's one of many stories about mythical hero Paul Bunyan, a giant lumberjack. Paul Bunyan became popular on the frontier in 1910. He starred in stories called "Tall Tales" for their exaggerated details, like the five huge storks that had to carry the gigantic baby Paul to his parents after he was born.

INDEX

Boldface indicates illustrations.

A
African civets 74, **74**
African wild dogs 68, **68**
Agoutis 52, **52**
Albatrosses 156, **156**
Alligators 30, **30**
Alpine ibex 108, **108**
Andean bears 53, **53**
Animal rescues
  bats 82–83, **83**
  black bears 18–19, **19**
  elephants 60–61, **61**
  lynx 104–105, **105**
  pandas 124–125, **124–125**
  penguins 144–145, **145**
  sea turtles 166–167, **167**
  sloths 38–39, **38–39**
Arctic foxes 142, **142**
Arctic hares 156, **156**
Arctic wolves 152, **152**
Armadillos 42, **42**

B
Bactrian camels 137, **137**
Badgers 109, **109**
Bald eagles 25, **25**
Bandicoots 96, **96**
Bats 82–83, **83**
Bears
  Andean bears 53, **53**
  black bears 18–19, **19**, 130, **131**
  brown bears **10–11**, 116, **116**
  giant pandas 124–125, **124–125**
  polar bears 146–147, **146–147**, 180–181
  sloth bears 137, **137**
Beavers 20, **20**
Bengal tigers 130, 131, **131**
Bighorn sheep 16–17, **16–17**
Bilbies 97, **97**
Binturongs 136, **136**
Biomes: world map 182–183
Bison 15, **15**, 117, **117**
Black bears 18–19, **19**, 130, **131**
Black-footed ferrets 30, **30**
Black swans 97, **97**
Blue-footed boobies 53, **53**
Bobcats 24, **24**
Bottlenose dolphins **158–159**, 164–165, **164–165**
Brown bears **10–11**, 116, **116**
Brown hares 103, **103**

C
Camels 137, **137**
Canada geese 156, **156**
Capybaras 43, **43**
Cassowaries 86, **86**
Cats
  bobcats 24, **24**
  cheetahs 66–67, **67**
  European wildcats 116, **116**
  fishing cats 136, **136**
  lions **54–55**, 58, **58**, 130, **131**
  lynx 104–105, **105**
  mountain lions 22, **23**
  ocelots 37, **37**
  sand cats 72–73, **72–73**
  snow leopards **118–119**, 134–135, **134–135**, 185
  tigers 130, 131, **131**

Chameleons 136, **136**
Chamois 116, **116**
Cheetahs 66–67, **67**
Chimpanzees 74, **74**
Chinchillas 53, **53**
Chipmunks 30, **30**
Civets 74, **74**
Clownfish 162, **162**
Coatis 53, **53**
Cobras 137, **137**
Coyotes 28–29, **28–29**
Crabs 178, **178**

D

Dall sheep 157, **157**
Dholes 137, **137**
Dik-diks 65, **65**
Dingoes 91, **91**
Dogs, domesticated 66, **67**, 110–111, **111**
Dolphins
    bottlenose dolphins **158–159**, 164–165, **164–165**
    orcas 172, **172**
    pink dolphins 48–49, **48–49**
Dormice 113, **113**

E

Eagles 25, **25**, 100–101, **101**
Echidnas 97, **97**
Eels 179, **179**
Elephant seals 150–151, **151**
Elephants 60–61, **61**
Emperor penguins 138, **138–139**, 144–145, **145**
Ermine 157, **157**
Eurasian badgers 109, **109**
Eurasian brown bears 116, **116**
European bee-eaters 117, **117**
European bison 117, **117**
European hedgehogs 102, **102**
European pine martens 117, **117**
European wildcats 116, **116**

F

Fennec foxes 75, **75**
Fischer's lovebirds 75, **75**
Fish 160–163, **161–163**, 168, **168**, 178, **178**, 179, **179**
Fishing cats 136, **136**
Folktales 27, 49, 71, 93, 115, 135, 155, 175, 184–185
Foxes
    arctic foxes 142, **142**
    fennec foxes 75, **75**
    red foxes 114, **114–115**
Friendships
    cheetah and dog 66–67, **67**
    kangaroo and wombat 88–89, **89**
    lambs and dog 110–111, **111**
    lion, tiger, and bear 130–131, **131**
    mountain lions and skunk 22–23, **23**
    sea lion at restaurant 170–171, **171**
    seal and penguin 150–151, **151**
    spider monkey and stuffed toys 44–45, **44–45**
Frogs 34–35, **35**, 96, **96**

G

Galápagos tortoises 52, **52**
Geckos 46, **46**
Geese 156, **156**
Gentoo penguins 150–151, **151**
Giant pandas 124–125, **124–125**
Giraffes 56–57, **57**
Golden brushtail possums 97, **97**
Gorillas 62–63, **62–63**
Great gray owls 116, **116**
Green tree frogs 96, **96**
Guanacos 40–41, **40–41**
Gundis 74, **74**

H

Hares
    arctic hares 156, **156**
    brown hares 103, **103**
Harp seals 141, **141**
Hedgehogs 98–99, 102, **102**
Hippopotamuses 59, **59**
Hummingbirds 30, **30**

I

Iberian lynx 104–105, **105**
Ibex 108, **108**
Indian paradise flycatchers 129, **129**

J

Japanese macaques 128, **128**
Jellyfish 178, **178**

K

Kangaroos 78–79, **79**, 88–89, **89**
Koalas **76–77**, 84–85, **84–85**
Komodo dragons 136, **136**
Kookaburras 92–93, **92–93**

L

Lemmings 157, **157**
Leopard tortoises 75, **75**
Lionfish 178, **178**
Lions **54–55**, 58, **58**, 130, **131**
Little penguins 90, **90**
Loggerhead turtles 166–167, **167**
Lovebirds 75, **75**
Lynx 104–105, **105**

M

Macaques 128, **128**
Manatees 173, **173**
Map 182–183
Marmosets 50–51, **50–51**
Meerkats 75, **75**
Monkeys
    Japanese macaques 128, **128**
    pygmy marmosets 50–51, **50–51**
    spider monkeys 44–45, **44–45**
Moose 157, **157**
Moray eels 179, **179**
Mountain lions 22, **23**
Musk oxen 156, **156**
Mustangs 21, **21**

N

Narwhals 178, **178**

O

Ocelots 37, **37**
Octopuses 169, **169**
Okapis 74, **74**
Olinguitos 52, **52**
Opossums 31, **31**
Orangutans 126–127, **126–127**
Orcas 172, **172**
Ostriches 69, **69**
Otters 176–177, **176–177**
Owls 31, **31**, 116, **116**, 148, **148**

P

Pandas 124–125, **124–125**
Penguins
    emperor penguins 138, **138–139**, 144–145, **145**
    gentoo penguins 150, 151, **151**
    little penguins 90, **90**
Piglet squid 179, **179**
Pine martens 117, **117**
Pink dolphins 48–49, **48–49**
Platypuses 87, **87**
Polar bears 146–147, **146–147**, 180–181
Porcupines 26–27, **26–27**
Prairie dogs 14, **14**
Pufferfish 168, **168**
Puffins 153, **153**
Pygmy marmosets 50–51, **50–51**

Q

Quokkas 80, **80**
Quolls 96, **96**

R

Rabbits 12–13, **13**
Raccoons 31, **31**
Red deer 112, **112**
Red foxes 114, **114–115**
Red pandas 123, **123**

Red squirrels 117, **117**
Reindeer 143, **143**
Rhinoceroses 120–121, **121**

S
Sand cats 72–73, **72–73**
Sea goldies 161, **161**
Sea lions 170–171, **171**
Sea otters 176–177, **176–177**
Sea stars 179, **179**
Sea turtles 166–167, **167**
Seahorses 163, **163**
Seals 140–141, **141**, 150, 151, **151**
Sheep
    bighorn sheep 16–17, **16–17**
    Dall sheep 157, **157**
    orphaned lambs 110, **111**
Skunks 22, 23, **23**
Sloth bears 137, **137**
Sloths **32–33**, 38–39, **38–39**
Slow lorises 122, **122**
Snow leopards **118–119**, 134–135,
    134–135, 185
Snowy owls 148, **148**
Spicebush swallowtails 31, **31**
Spider monkeys 44–45, **44–45**
Squid 179, **179**
Squirrels 117, **117**
Steppe eagles 101, **101**
Stingrays 179, **179**
Sugar gliders 81, **81**
Swans 97, **97**

T
Tamanduas 36, **36**
Tapirs 47, **47**
Tarsiers 132, **132**
Tasmanian devils 94–95, **94–95**
Tigers 130, 131, **131**
Tortoises
    Galápagos tortoises 52, **52**
    leopard tortoises 75, **75**

Toucans 52, **52**
Tree frogs 96, **96**
Tree kangaroos 96, **96**
Turtles 166–167, **167**

W
Walruses 154–155, **154–155**
Warthogs 64, **64**
Weasels 106–107, **106–107**
Whales 174–175, **174–175**
Wolverines 149, **149**
Wolves 111, 152, **152**
Wombats 88–89, **89**

Y
Yaks 133, **133**

Z
Zebras 70–71, **70–71**

INDEX OF POEMS

"The Duck and the Kangaroo" 78
"The Eagle (A fragment)" 100
"Frog Ballet" 34
"The Giraffe" 56
"Good Morning" 8
"The Pet Rabbit" 12
"The Rhinoceros" 120
"Seal Lullaby" 140
"Till To-Morrow." 180
"We Fish" 160

PHOTO CREDITS

Dust Jacket: Front cover (UP LE), Jan Vermeer/Minden Pictures; (UP CTR), Elizabeth DeLaney/Getty Images; (UP RT), Sam Trull; (CTR LE), Beverly Joubert/National Geographic Creative; (CTR RT), Mohd Rasfan/Getty Images; (LO LE), Hanneke Luijting/Getty Images; (LO CTR), Nature Picture Library/Alamy Stock Photo; Back cover, Norbert Rosing/National Geographic Creative; Spine, Donald M. Jones/Minden Pictures; Front flap, Lisa & Mike Husar/TeamHusar.com; Back flap, Thomas Kitchin and Victoria Hurst/Leeson Photo; **Case:** Front cover, Terry Whittaker/Getty Images; Back cover, WorldsWildlifeWonders/Shutterstock; 1, Suzi Eszterhas/Minden Pictures; 2, Arterra/UIG via Getty Images; 7 (UP LE), Ondreicka/Dreamstime; 7 (UP CTR), Sharon Heald/NPL/Minden Pictures; 7 (UP RT), Tierfotoagentur/Alamy Stock Photo; 7 (CTR LE), W. Lynch/ArcticPhoto; 7 (CTR CTR), Suzan Meldonian/SeaPics.com; 7 (CTR RT), Bob Smith/National Geographic Creative; 7 (LO LE), Xavier Eichaker/Biosphoto; 7 (LO CTR), Matthias Breiter/Minden Pictures; 7 (LO RT), Konrad Wothe/Minden Pictures; 9, Lisa & Mike Husar/TeamHusar.com; 11, Deb Garside/Getty Images; 13, Patrice Correia/Biosphoto; 14, Tom Reichner/Shutterstock; 15, Sumio Harada/Minden Pictures; 16, Bird Images/Getty Images; 17, Jeff Vanuga/Getty Images; 19 (UP), Appalachian Bear Rescue; 19 (LO), Appalachian Bear Rescue; 20, Holly Kuchera/Shutterstock; 21, Klein-Hubert/Kimball Stock; 23 (UP LE), Animals of Montana; 23 (LO RT), Animals of Montana; 24, Lisa & Mike Husar/TeamHusar.com; 25, Art Wolfe/artwolfe.com; 26, Debbie Steinhausser/Alamy Stock Photo; 28, Lisa & Mike Husar/TeamHusar.com; 29, Lisa & Mike Husar/TeamHusar.com; 30 (UP LE), Will E. Davis/Shutterstock; 30 (UP RT), Rick & Nora Bowers/Alamy Stock Photo; 30 (LO RT), Jad Images/Shutterstock; 30 (LO LE), Sylvain Cordier/Biosphoto; 31 (UP LE), tlindsayg/Getty Images; 31 (UP RT), Richard Seeley/Getty Images; 31 (LO RT), stanley45/Getty Images; 31 (LO LE), Heiko Kiera/Shutterstock; 33, Suzi Eszterhas/Minden Pictures; 35, Thomas Kitchin & Victoria Hurst/Leeson Photo; 36, Sam Trull; 37, Roy Toft/National Geographic Creative; 38, Sam Trull; 39 (UP), Sam Trull; 39 (LO), Sam Trull; 40-41, Mint Images/Art Wolfe/Getty Images; 42, Tierfotoagentur/Alamy Stock Photo; 43, Nature Picture Library/Alamy Stock Photo; 44, James D. Morgan/REX/Shutterstock; 45 (UP), James D. Morgan/REX/Shutterstock; 45 (CTR RT), Coppel/Newspix/REX/Shutterstock; 45 (LO), James D. Morgan/REX/Shutterstock; 46, Animals/SuperStock; 47, Ben Queenborough/Getty Images; 48, Sylvain Cordier/Getty Images; 50, Thomas Marent/ardea.com; 51, DmitriMaruta/Getty Images; 52 (UP LE), Sylvain Cordier/Biosphoto; 52 (UP RT), Photo by Mark Gurney for Smithsonian via Getty Images; 52 (LO RT), Pete Oxford/Minden Pictures; 52 (LO LE), Haroldo Palo Jr/NHPA/Photoshot; 53 (UP LE), ZSSD/Minden Pictures; 53 (UP RT), Thomas Kitchin & Victoria Hurst/Leeson Photo; 53 (LO RT), Philip Dalton/Minden Pictures; 53 (LO LE), Tui De Roy/Minden Pictures; 55, Richard Du Toit/Minden Pictures; 57, Richard Du Toit/Minden Pictures; 58, Jonathan & Angela Scott/Getty Images; 59, Mike Wilkes/Minden Pictures; 61 (LE), David Sheldrick Wildlife Trust; 61 (RT), David Sheldrick Wildlife Trust; 62, Suzi Eszterhas/Minden Pictures; 63, Eric Baccega/Minden Pictures; 64, Nature Picture Library/Alamy Stock Photo; 65, Fotosearch/Getty Images; 67 (LE), Busch Gardens Tampa Bay/Barcroft Media Ltd.; 67 (RT), Barcroft USA/Barcroft Media via Getty Images; 68, Manoj Shah/Getty Images; 69, Ignacio Yufera/Biosphoto; 70, age fotostock/Alamy Stock Photo; 72-73, Xavier Eichaker/Biosphoto; 74 (UP LE), Anup Shah/Nature Picture Library; 74 (UP RT), Laurent Geslin/Nature Picture Library; 74 (LO RT), Arco Images GmbH/Kimball Stock; 74 (LO LE), Henning Kaiser/Picture Alliance/Photoshot; 75 (UP LE), Floridapfe from S.Korea Kim in cherl/Getty Images; 75 (UP RT), Will Burrard-Lucas/Nature Picture Library; 75 (LO RT), Hemis/Alamy Stock Photo; 75 (LO LE), Arco Images GmbH/Alamy Stock

For Parker and Kassy. —SWD

Since 1888, the National Geographic Society has funded more than 12,000 research, exploration, and preservation projects around the world. The Society receives funds from National Geographic Partners, LLC, funded in part by your purchase. A portion of the proceeds from this book supports this vital work. To learn more, visit natgeo.com/info.

For more information, visit nationalgeographic.com, call 1-800-647-5463, or write to the following address:

National Geographic Partners
1145 17th Street N.W.
Washington, D.C. 20036-4688 U.S.A.

Visit us online at nationalgeographic.com/books

For librarians and teachers: ngchildrensbooks.org

More for kids from National Geographic:
kids.nationalgeographic.com

For information about special discounts for bulk purchases, please contact National Geographic Books Special Sales: specialsales@natgeo.com

For rights or permissions inquiries, please contact National Geographic Books Subsidiary Rights: bookrights@natgeo.com

Library of Congress Cataloging-in-Publication Data

Names: Drimmer, Stephanie Warren.
Title: Hey, baby! / Stephanie Drimmer.
Description: Washington, D.C. : National Geographic
    Kids, 2017.
Identifiers: LCCN 2017010528| ISBN 9781426329319
    (hardcover : alk. paper) | ISBN 9781426329326
    (hardcover : alk. paper)
Subjects: LCSH: Animals--Infancy--Pictorial works--
    Juvenile literature. | Photography of infants--Juvenile
    literature.
Classification: LCC QL763 .D75 2017 | DDC 591.3/92--dc23
LC record available at https://lccn.loc.gov/2017010528

Designed by Amanda Larsen

The publisher would like to thank everyone who made this book possible: Becky Baines, executive editor; Jen Agresta, project editor; Paige Towler, contributing writer; Sarah J. Mock, senior photo editor; Mary Jo Courchesne, rights clearance; Sally Abbey, managing editor; Joan Gossett, editorial production manager; Gus Tello and Anne LeongSon, production designers.

Printed in China
17/PPS/1